THE EVOLUTION OF CONSCIOUSNESS

BY STORMRIDER

THE EVOLUTION OF CONSCIOUSNESS

First edition. December 22, 2024.

ISBN: 979-8230802891

Written by Stormrider.

Table of Contents

A Note to the Reader

Dear Reader,

You hold in your hands not just a book, but a map to the territories of human potential. This work represents decades of research, countless hours of observation, and the collected wisdom of researchers and practitioners from around the world. Yet it is, at its heart, a deeply personal journey—one that each reader will experience in their own unique way.

As you navigate these pages, you'll encounter various frameworks, methodologies, and insights. Some may resonate immediately, while others might challenge your existing perspectives. This is not just natural—it's essential to the transformative process. Each chapter builds upon the previous ones, creating a comprehensive understanding of human potential and consciousness evolution.

A few suggestions for approaching this work:

1. Take your time. The concepts presented here are meant to be experienced and integrated, not merely understood intellectually.
2. Trust your intuition about which sections to explore deeply at any given time. While the chapters progress logically, you may find yourself drawn to certain areas that align with your current growth edges.
3. Consider keeping a journal of your insights and questions. The true value of this work often emerges through personal reflection and application.
4. Remember that transformation is not linear. You may find yourself revisiting earlier chapters with new understanding as you progress.
5. Connect with others exploring similar territories. While personal growth is unique to each individual, sharing experiences and insights can enrich the journey.

The methodologies and frameworks presented here are not meant to be prescriptive but rather to illuminate possibilities. They are invitations to explore your own potential in ways that honor your unique nature while connecting you to universal principles of human development.

This book represents not an endpoint but a beginning—a gateway to continuing exploration of human potential. The greatest discoveries may be the ones you make as you apply these insights to your own journey of growth and transformation.

May this work serve as both mirror and window—reflecting your own potential while opening new vistas of possibility.

With deepest appreciation for your commitment to growth and discovery.

Chapter 1: The Origins of Ambition

1.1 Roots of Desire

The first memory Elena Rodriguez could recall was not of warmth or comfort, but of tension—a quiet, persistent undercurrent that vibrated through the small, cramped apartment her family called home. It was the sound of her father's measured breathing as he pored over engineering textbooks late into the night, his calloused fingers tracing diagrams while the rest of the world slumbered.

Maria and Carlos Rodriguez were not people who believed in idle dreams. They were survivors, immigrants who had crossed borders with nothing but hope and an unbreakable determination to carve out a better life for their children. Carlos, a mechanical engineer who had been forced to work as a construction laborer in this new country, never spoke of the technical degrees that hung—dusty and faded—in their tiny hallway. Those papers represented a past life, a professional identity stripped away by circumstance and the brutal realities of immigration.

Elena would later understand that her father's nightly studies were more than mere nostalgia. They were an act of resistance, a quiet rebellion against a system that had deemed him expendable. Each highlighted textbook page, each carefully annotated margin was a testament to his refusal to be defined by his current occupation.

Her mother, Maria, was equally complex. A former accountant in their home country, she now worked double shifts as a hospital cleaner and seamstress. Her hands, perpetually marked by industrial cleaning chemicals and needle pricks, told a story of sacrifice that Elena would only fully comprehend years later. Maria's conversations were rarely about what was, but always about what could be—a subtle distinction that would profoundly shape Elena's understanding of potential.

"Potential," Maria would often say, her voice a mixture of warning and hope, "is not something given. It is something you claim."

The Rodriguez household existed in a delicate balance between survival and aspiration. Every resource was calculated, every opportunity scrutinized.

There was no room for frivolity, but also no absence of love. Their version of love was pragmatic—demonstrated through strategic sacrifices, carefully planned educations, and an unwavering belief that the next generation would transcend the limitations of the current one.

1.2 Early Stirrings of Aspiration

Elena's childhood was not marked by traditional markers of success. Their neighborhood, a dense, multicultural enclave on the edges of the city, was a mosaic of similar stories—families holding onto dreams with a tenacity that bordered on desperate hope.

From an early age, Elena recognized that knowledge was the most valuable currency in her world. While other children collected toys, she collected information. The local library became her sanctuary, a place where social constraints dissolved and intellectual boundaries seemed permeable. She devoured books across disciplines—engineering manuals that reminded her of her father's studies, economic treatises that echoed her mother's precise financial planning, and novels that offered glimpses into worlds beyond her immediate reality.

Her teachers quickly recognized something distinctive about Elena. She wasn't just intelligent; she was strategically curious. Unlike her peers who absorbed information passively, she interrogated every piece of knowledge, understanding instinctively that information was a tool to be wielded, not merely consumed.

Mr. Thompson, her high school economics teacher, was the first adult outside her family who truly saw her. During a class discussion about socioeconomic mobility, while other students offered generic responses, Elena presented a nuanced analysis that combined statistical data with personal narrative. She spoke about immigration, labor markets, and systemic barriers with a clarity that belied her age.

"You're not just answering the question," Mr. Thompson told her after class. "You're reframing the entire conversation."

It was a pivotal moment. Elena realized that her aspirations couldn't be confined to traditional definitions of success. She wasn't just seeking a career; she was mapping a strategy for transformation—not just for herself, but potentially for her entire community.

1.3 The First Glimpse of Possibility

The moment of true awakening came during her sophomore year of high school. A visiting tech entrepreneur spoke about innovation, not as an abstract concept, but as a tool for social change. His presentation wasn't just about technological advancement; it was about using knowledge as a mechanism for disrupting established systems.

Elena sat in the auditorium, her notebook filled not just with notes, but with interconnected diagrams—mapping potential pathways, identifying systemic vulnerabilities, envisioning strategies of intervention. She wasn't just listening; she was strategizing.

That evening, she shared her insights with her parents. Carlos and Maria listened—not with the dismissive patience many parents might offer, but with a profound, almost electric attentiveness. They recognized in their daughter something beyond ambition: a nascent revolutionary spirit tempered by strategic thinking.

"Remember," her father said, his voice soft but intense, "power is not given. It is constructed, carefully and deliberately."

Her mother added, with a characteristic blend of pragmatism and hope, "And reconstruction begins with understanding."

As the city outside their apartment window transitioned from the golden hues of sunset to the steely blues of night, Elena understood that her journey was about more than personal achievement. It was about creating blueprints of possibility—for herself, for her family, for her community.

The roots of her ambition were not planted in grand gestures, but in these quiet, profound moments of recognition. She was not just a daughter of immigrants; she was becoming an architect of transformation.

Her story was just beginning.

Chapter 2: Social Landscape of Opportunity

2.1 Navigating Class Boundaries

The community center stood as a testament to resilience, its faded brick walls holding stories of countless immigrants who had passed through its doors. On this crisp autumn morning, it hummed with a quiet intensity that Elena Rodriguez had come to understand intimately—a soundscape of aspiration, struggle, and unspoken dreams.

Her mother's words echoed in her mind: "Boundaries are not walls. They are puzzles waiting to be solved."

The community center's evening education program had been Elena's lifeline, a bridge between the world she was born into and the world she was determined to create. Here, among fellow first-generation students, immigrants, and children of working-class families, she learned that social constraints were less about limitations and more about strategic navigation.

Maria Rodriguez had been her first lesson in social maneuvering. Elena remembered watching her mother transform herself between contexts—the submissive hospital cleaner during work hours, the fierce, strategic planner at home, the respected community leader during neighborhood meetings. Each iteration was a careful performance, a nuanced dance of survival and ambition.

"Observation is your most powerful tool," her mother would say. "Before you challenge a system, you must understand its intricate mechanisms."

The evening classes were more than educational opportunities. They were intricate social laboratories where students like Elena learned to decode the unwritten rules of social mobility. Professor Ramirez, a sociologist who had himself navigated multiple social landscapes, became a crucial mentor.

"Social mobility isn't about erasing your origins," he would explain, his eyes holding a mixture of wisdom and challenge. "It's about understanding how to translate your unique experiences into universal languages of opportunity."

2.2 Unspoken Rules of Advancement

Elena's world was defined by a complex negotiation of cultural expectations. Her immigrant community held simultaneously contradictory expectations—complete assimilation and fierce preservation of cultural identity, economic success and collective solidarity, individual ambition and family responsibility.

The Rodriguez family embodied these contradictions. Her father, Carlos, had sacrificed his professional engineering credentials, working construction jobs to provide stability. Yet, he insisted on maintaining the intellectual rigor of his original profession, studying engineering manuals every evening, refusing to let his professional identity be completely erased.

Her mother, Maria, was a master of cultural navigation. She spoke perfect English with a slight accent that she strategically modulated—softening it in professional settings, embracing it in community spaces. She understood that language was more than communication; it was a tool of social positioning.

Elena was learning to become a similar cultural architect. She didn't just move between social worlds; she created bridges, translating experiences, building networks that transcended traditional boundaries.

The community center's adult education program became her first true laboratory of social strategy. Here, she met individuals from diverse backgrounds—recent immigrants, working-class adults seeking career transformations, refugees rebuilding their lives.

Rosa Martinez, a hospital administrator pursuing additional certifications, became a close friend and strategic ally. Their conversations were masterclasses in understanding social dynamics.

"It's not about fitting in," Rosa would say during their study sessions. "It's about creating spaces where you can authentically exist while strategically advancing."

2.3 Mapping the Path of Ambition

Strategic positioning became Elena's most refined skill. She understood that social advancement was a complex chess game, requiring multiple simultaneous strategies.

Her approach was methodical. She didn't just attend classes; she analyzed them. Who were the instructors? What were their backgrounds? What unspoken networks existed beneath the surface of formal education?

Professor James Thompson, a sociologist specializing in social mobility, became an unexpected mentor. During a small group discussion about systemic barriers, Elena presented an analysis that was part academic research, part personal narrative.

"You're not just describing barriers," Thompson told her after class. "You're mapping potential pathways of transformation."

His observation was pivotal. Elena began to see social constraints not as immovable obstacles but as complex systems with inherent vulnerabilities. Each social barrier was a puzzle waiting to be strategically decoded.

Her network grew intentionally. She wasn't collecting contacts; she was building an ecosystem of mutual advancement. Study groups became strategic alliances. Classroom discussions transformed into potential professional collaborations.

The Rodriguez family's approach to education had always been about more than individual achievement. It was a collective strategy of social elevation. Every educational milestone was a victory not just for the individual, but for the entire community.

Elena's older brother, Miguel, had been the first to attend college, breaking ground for her own journey. His path had been fraught with challenges—working multiple jobs, navigating financial aid systems, balancing family responsibilities with academic pursuits.

"We're not just studying," Miguel would tell her. "We're creating blueprints for those who will follow."

Her high school guidance counselor had been skeptical initially. Another statistic, another immigrant kid with big dreams. But Elena's approach was different. She didn't just dream; she strategized. Scholarship applications became carefully crafted narratives. Internship opportunities were meticulously researched and pursued.

By her senior year, she had not just succeeded academically. She had begun to redefine what success looked like for her community.

The social landscape was not a fixed terrain. It was a living, breathing ecosystem of possibilities. And Elena was learning to be its architect.

As the community center's evening lights flickered on, casting long shadows across the room, Elena understood that her journey was about more than personal achievement. It was about creating new maps of possibility for those who would follow.

The boundaries were shifting. And she was at the center of that transformation.

Chapter 3: The Awakening of Passion

3.1 Emotional Crossroads

The university library was Elena's sanctuary, a cathedral of possibility where the boundaries between intellectual pursuit and personal transformation blurred into something profound and indefinable. Late-night study sessions had become more than academic rituals—they were moments of deep introspection, where the carefully constructed walls of her strategic self began to show unexpected fissures.

Marcus Chen sat two tables away, his profile illuminated by the soft glow of a research laptop. Elena had noticed him before—not just for his striking appearance, but for the intensity with which he engaged with his work. He was different from the typical engineering students she knew. There was a philosophical depth to his approach that transcended mere technical proficiency.

Her internal landscape was a complex terrain of conflicting emotions. The Rodriguez family's narrative had always been about strategic survival, about channeling passion into purposeful action. Emotional exploration was a luxury they had never afforded themselves. Yet here she was, feeling something that defied her meticulously planned worldview.

The conflict was not new. Throughout her academic journey, Elena had learned to compartmentalize. Emotions were not to be indulged but analyzed, understood, and strategically managed. Her mother's lessons echoed in her mind: "Passion without direction is like a river without banks—destructive and ultimately wasted."

But something was changing. The rigid boundaries she had constructed were beginning to feel more like self-imposed prison walls than protective strategies.

Her research project on urban technological innovation had become more than an academic pursuit. It was a deeply personal exploration of transformation—not just of cities, but of human potential. Each data point, each interview, each analytical framework felt like a piece of a much larger puzzle of human experience.

Marcus looked up, catching her gaze. There was no awkwardness in the moment, just a sudden, electric recognition of something unspoken.

3.2 Desire Beyond Circumstance

Their first real conversation happened unexpectedly. A complex modeling problem that had been frustrating Elena for weeks suddenly found resolution through an impromptu collaborative discussion.

"You're not just solving a problem," Marcus observed, his fingers tracing algorithmic solutions on a shared notebook. "You're reimagining the entire approach."

Elena recognized in Marcus something rare—an intellectual equal who saw beyond traditional boundaries. He was the son of Chinese immigrants, a technological innovator who understood the complex intersections of culture, technology, and human potential.

Their conversations became intellectual dance—challenging, provocative, deeply intimate without physical proximity. Marcus wasn't just intelligent; he was philosophically radical. His approach to technology was fundamentally humanitarian, seeing innovation as a tool for social transformation rather than mere technical achievement.

"Technology isn't neutral," he would argue during their late-night discussions. "It's a language of human potential, a mechanism for reimagining social structures."

Elena found herself simultaneously attracted to and challenged by Marcus. He represented a different kind of ambition—one that wasn't about personal achievement but collective transformation.

Her family's history of survival had taught her to be cautious. Romantic entanglements were potential distractions from the larger mission of social mobility. Yet, with Marcus, something felt different. He wasn't a distraction. He was a potential collaborator in a much larger vision.

The tension was palpable—intellectual, emotional, unspoken. Each interaction felt like a careful negotiation of boundaries, a dance of mutual recognition and strategic vulnerability.

3.3 Breaking Personal Limitations

The turning point came during a collaborative research project on urban resilience. Marcus and Elena's approach was unconventional, combining technological modeling with deep sociological insights.

Their work caught the attention of Dr. Elena Kaplan, a renowned urban innovation expert. "You're not just analyzing urban systems," she told them during a critical presentation. "You're proposing a fundamental reimagining of how human communities interact with technological infrastructure."

The project became more than an academic exercise. It was a manifestation of their shared vision—technology as a mechanism of human empowerment, innovation as a pathway to social transformation.

Elena began to understand that her previous approach to ambition had been fundamentally limited. Survival was not enough. Transformation required a more holistic understanding of human potential.

Her conversations with Marcus became increasingly personal. He spoke of his parents' journey—how they had navigated multiple cultural landscapes, how innovation had been their primary language of survival and aspiration.

"We are not defined by our circumstances," he would say. "We are defined by our capacity to reimagine them."

The Rodriguez family's narrative of survival had been about strategic navigation. Marcus introduced her to a different paradigm—one of creative reimagination.

Her mother noticed the change. During a weekend family dinner, Maria Rodriguez studied her daughter with a mixture of curiosity and understanding.

"You are finding your own path," she observed, her voice holding both a question and a statement.

Elena realized that passion was not a distraction from her mission. It was the mission's most profound fuel.

The boundaries between personal and professional, between emotional and strategic, began to dissolve. She was becoming something more than she had originally conceived—not just an individual pursuing success, but a potential architect of broader social transformation.

Marcus represented more than a romantic possibility. He was a philosophical collaborator, a mirror reflecting dimensions of herself she was just beginning to understand.

As the university campus transformed around her, bathed in the soft light of emerging possibility, Elena Rodriguez understood that her journey was just beginning.

Passion was not a weakness to be controlled. It was a powerful, transformative energy waiting to be strategically unleashed.

Chapter 4: Strategies of Social Climbing

4.1 Intellectual Weaponry

The conference hall buzzed with a carefully curated energy—a blend of academic prestige, technological innovation, and unspoken social hierarchies. Elena Rodriguez moved through the space like a strategic chess player, each conversation a calculated move, each interaction a potential pathway to broader opportunities.

Her preparation for this moment had been years in the making. The Urban Innovation Summit was more than a professional conference. It was a battlefield of intellectual positioning, where careers were made, networks were forged, and social boundaries were negotiated.

Marcus stood nearby, their collaborative research paper tucked carefully in a portfolio that represented months of intense work. They had discovered something profound—a new framework for understanding urban technological resilience that challenged existing academic paradigms.

Elena remembered her father's lessons about professional survival. "Knowledge is not just what you know," Carlos Rodriguez would say, his engineering manuals spread across their small apartment's dining table. "It's how you use what you know to create possibility."

Her approach was methodical. She had studied not just the conference's official program, but the intricate social networks that existed beneath the surface. Who were the key influencers? What were the unspoken alliances? What intellectual vulnerabilities could be strategically addressed?

Dr. Elena Kaplan, a renowned urban innovation expert, approached their presentation area. Her reputation preceded her—a formidable intellectual who had transformed multiple academic disciplines.

"Your research challenges fundamental assumptions," Kaplan observed, her keen eyes dissecting their work. "But challenging isn't enough. You must offer a compelling alternative narrative."

It was a masterclass in intellectual maneuvering. Elena understood that knowledge was a complex currency—its value determined not just by content, but by strategic presentation.

4.2 Connections and Manipulations

Networking was an art form Elena had been studying her entire life. Growing up in an immigrant community, she had observed how social connections could be lifelines, how information and relationships could transform limitations into opportunities.

The conference was a living ecosystem of potential. Each conversation was a carefully negotiated exchange—not just of words, but of intellectual and social capital.

Marcus watched her with a mixture of admiration and fascination. "You're not just presenting research," he whispered during a break. "You're conducting a complex social negotiation."

Her strategy was multilayered. She didn't just seek connections; she created ecosystems of mutual advancement. A conversation with a junior researcher could be as valuable as an interaction with a senior academic. Each connection was a potential bridge, each relationship a strategic investment.

Rosa Martinez, her longtime friend from the community center, had taught her an important lesson. "Networking isn't about collecting business cards," Rosa would say. "It's about understanding human potential."

Elena's approach went beyond traditional networking. She was building what she conceptualized as an "opportunity network"—a dynamic, interconnected system where knowledge, resources, and potential could flow organically.

Her family's immigrant background had been her first lesson in strategic connection. Watching her parents navigate complex social landscapes—translating not just language, but cultural nuances—had been her most profound education.

4.3 The Art of Calculated Charm

Charm, Elena had learned, was a precisely calibrated instrument. It wasn't about superficial charisma, but about creating genuine moments of human connection while maintaining strategic clarity.

Dr. James Rodriguez—no relation, but a key figure in urban policy research—became a crucial connection. Their conversation began with their research but quickly evolved into a nuanced discussion about social innovation.

"You're not just proposing technical solutions," he observed. "You're reimagining social infrastructure."

Elena understood the power of such moments. Each interaction was an opportunity to reframe narratives, to challenge existing paradigms.

Her mother's lessons echoed in her approach. Maria Rodriguez had been a master of social navigation, able to move between different cultural and professional spaces with remarkable fluidity.

"Charm is about making people feel seen," Maria would say. "Not just heard, but truly understood."

The conference became a complex dance of intellectual and social positioning. Elena wasn't just presenting research. She was conducting a sophisticated social experiment, testing the boundaries of professional advancement.

Marcus complemented her approach perfectly. Where she was strategic and precise, he brought a philosophical depth that transformed their interactions from mere networking to genuine intellectual exploration.

Their collaborative presentation was a testament to their approach. It wasn't just a research paper. It was a reimagining of how urban technological systems could address complex social challenges.

Dr. Kaplan's response was pivotal. "You're not just proposing a technical solution," she told them after their presentation. "You're offering a new language of urban transformation."

The recognition was more than professional validation. It was an acknowledgment that they were creating new pathways of understanding.

As the conference progressed, Elena realized that social climbing was not about climbing a predetermined ladder. It was about reimagining the entire concept of professional advancement.

Her strategy went beyond individual achievement. She was creating ecosystems of opportunity, building bridges between different professional and cultural landscapes.

The Rodriguez family's narrative of survival had been about strategic navigation. But Elena was developing something more profound—a approach to professional and social transformation that saw barriers as opportunities for creative reimagination.

The conference hall continued to buzz with conversations, with exchanges of ideas and potential. And at its center, Elena Rodriguez stood—not just as a participant, but as a potential architect of new social possibilities.

Charm, intelligence, strategy—these were not just tools. They were languages of transformation.

Chapter 5: Romantic Entanglements

5.1 First Significant Encounter

The urban innovation conference had been more than a professional milestone—it was a transformative moment that reverberated through every aspect of Elena Rodriguez's life. The connections she had forged, the intellectual boundaries she had challenged, now seemed to pulse with an energy that extended far beyond academic circles.

Gabriel Torres entered her life like an unexpected theorem—complex, nuanced, and challenging every preconceived notion she had about professional and personal boundaries.

He was not the typical academic Elena had encountered. A policy strategist with the city's urban development bureau, Gabriel moved through professional spaces with a fluidity that was both intriguing and slightly unsettling. Where Elena was methodical and strategic, he seemed to operate on a more intuitive wavelength—yet their initial interaction suggested a profound intellectual resonance.

Their first substantive conversation occurred during a post-conference reception, an liminal space where professional networking dissolved into more personal exchanges. The venue was a minimalist gallery in the city's emerging arts district—exposed brick walls, industrial lighting, and floor-to-ceiling windows that offered a panoramic view of the urban landscape they both sought to understand and transform.

"Your research on technological resilience," Gabriel said, his voice carrying a tone that was both analytical and deeply curious, "it's not just about infrastructure. You're proposing a philosophy of urban adaptation."

Elena recognized immediately that this was not a standard professional compliment. It was an invitation to a deeper dialogue, a recognition of the underlying conceptual framework that drove her work.

"Adaptation is survival," she responded, watching his eyes—sharp, intelligent, holding a complexity that suggested multiple layers of understanding. "Whether we're talking about technological systems or human communities, the capacity to evolve is fundamental."

Their conversation became a delicate dance of intellectual sparring. Gabriel challenged her assumptions not to undermine, but to explore. He presented alternative perspectives that didn't feel like opposition, but like collaborative problem-solving.

"You see cities as living organisms," he observed. "Not static structures, but dynamic ecosystems with their own logic of survival and growth."

It was more than a discussion about urban planning. It was a metaphorical exploration of human potential, of how systems—whether technological, social, or emotional—could be reimagined.

What Elena didn't immediately recognize was how this intellectual connection would become a catalyst for a more profound personal transformation.

5.2 Passion vs. Pragmatism

The weeks following the conference became a complex negotiation between professional ambition and emerging emotional terrain.

Gabriel represented a different approach to professional and personal advancement. Where Elena's strategy had always been precise and calculated, he seemed to operate from a space of intuitive connection—understanding systems not just through analytical frameworks, but through empathetic engagement.

Their subsequent meetings—ostensibly professional consultations about urban innovation strategies—carried an undercurrent of something more nuanced. Each interaction challenged Elena's carefully constructed boundaries between personal and professional domains.

Her family history had taught her the importance of strategic navigation. Carlos and Maria Rodriguez had survived and ultimately thrived by understanding that every interaction was an opportunity, every relationship a potential pathway to broader possibilities.

But Gabriel was different. He didn't see relationships as transactional networks to be strategically managed. For him, connection was intrinsic, valuable in and of itself.

"You approach everything like a complex algorithm," he told her during one of their working sessions, a hint of both admiration and gentle critique in his voice. "But human systems aren't just about optimization. They're about understanding."

The statement resonated in a way that made Elena uncomfortable. Her entire professional approach had been about creating predictive models, about understanding complex urban systems through rational frameworks. Yet Gabriel suggested there were dimensions of human experience that transcended pure rationality.

Her conversations with Marcus—her research collaborator—took on a reflective tone.

"He challenges your entire methodology," Marcus observed. "Not by attacking it, but by suggesting there are alternative ways of knowing."

The dilemma was profound. Could her carefully constructed professional identity accommodate this more fluid, emotionally intelligent approach? Or would engaging with Gabriel mean compromising the strategic precision that had been her strength?

5.3 Love as a Strategic Asset

Elena began to understand that her emerging connection with Gabriel was not a deviation from her strategic approach to life, but potentially its most sophisticated manifestation.

Their relationship became an intellectual and emotional collaboration. Gabriel's work in urban policy complemented her technological research in ways that were more than merely professional. Together, they were developing a holistic approach to understanding urban transformation—one that integrated technological innovation, social dynamics, and human potential.

Rosa Martinez—her longtime friend from the community center—observed the transformation with a knowing smile.

"You're not just falling in love," Rosa told her. "You're creating a new paradigm of professional and personal integration."

The observation was profoundly accurate. Elena was discovering that emotional connection, when approached with the same strategic intelligence she applied to her professional work, could be an extraordinary catalyst for growth.

Gabriel introduced her to networks and perspectives she hadn't previously considered. His connections in policy circles complemented her technological expertise, creating a synergistic approach to urban innovation that was greater than the sum of its individual parts.

Their relationship became a strategic partnership—not in a calculated, transactional sense, but as a genuine collaboration of intellect and emotion.

During a joint presentation at a urban policy symposium, their complementary approaches became evident. Where Elena presented complex technological frameworks, Gabriel articulated the human and social implications, creating a narrative of urban transformation that was both intellectually rigorous and deeply empathetic.

"We're not just solving technical challenges," Gabriel would say, his hand occasionally brushing Elena's in a gesture that was both professional and intimately connected. "We're reimagining the very concept of urban living."

Her mother's wisdom echoed in these moments. "True power," Maria Rodriguez had always said, "comes from understanding that personal and professional growth are not separate journeys, but interconnected landscapes."

Elena was living that wisdom now. Her relationship with Gabriel was not a distraction from her professional ambitions, but an extraordinary extension of them.

The strategic approach that had defined her entire life was evolving. No longer was it about climbing predetermined ladders or navigating fixed social hierarchies. It was about creating new possibilities, about understanding that personal transformation and professional advancement were part of a holistic journey of growth.

As the urban landscape continued to shift and transform around them, Elena and Gabriel stood as collaborative architects—not just of technological systems, but of new ways of understanding human potential.

Their love was not a deviation from her strategic life. It was its most sophisticated expression.

Chapter 6: The Cost of Ambition

6.1 Moral Compromises

The invitation arrived on cream-colored cardstock, embossed with the letterhead of Nexus Innovations—a technology conglomerate known for its groundbreaking urban development projects and equally notorious for its complex ethical landscape. For Elena Rodriguez, it represented both an extraordinary opportunity and a profound moral crossroads.

The research proposal was elegant in its complexity: develop predictive algorithms for urban infrastructure that could potentially revolutionize city planning. The funding was substantial—enough to transform her entire research trajectory, to provide resources for her team, to create opportunities that had previously seemed impossible.

But the ethical implications were anything but straightforward.

The algorithms Nexus proposed would leverage unprecedented levels of data collection. Traffic patterns, energy consumption, personal movement trajectories—all would be integrated into a comprehensive urban mapping system. The potential benefits were clear: more efficient resource allocation, improved urban design, enhanced emergency response capabilities.

The potential risks, however, were equally profound.

Elena found herself in her home office, surrounded by the accumulated evidence of her professional journey. Photographs of her family—Carlos and Maria Rodriguez, standing proudly in front of their first apartment in the immigrant neighborhood—watched her from the wall. Their story of survival, of strategic navigation through complex social landscapes, seemed to whisper urgent questions.

Marcus, her longtime research collaborator, had been unequivocal during their late-night discussion.

"This is more than a technical challenge," he said, his voice carrying the weight of deep ethical consideration. "We're talking about a system that could fundamentally reshape individual privacy. Every movement, every choice could become a data point to be analyzed, predicted, potentially manipulated."

Gabriel, whose perspective had become increasingly important in her decision-making process, offered a more nuanced view.

"The question isn't whether the technology is possible," he argued. "The question is who controls it, and to what end."

Her father's lessons about professional survival echoed in her mind. "Opportunities are not just given," Carlos would say. "They are created, negotiated, sometimes wrestled from seemingly impossible circumstances."

But this opportunity demanded more than professional negotiation. It demanded a fundamental examination of her ethical framework.

The research could provide unprecedented insights into urban resilience. It could help communities better prepare for environmental challenges, optimize resource distribution, create more responsive urban infrastructures.

It could also become a tool of unprecedented social control.

Elena understood that her decision would not just impact her professional trajectory. It would be a statement about the kind of technological future she believed was possible.

6.2 Personal Sacrifices

The moral deliberation took its psychological toll. Elena found herself experiencing a profound sense of internal fragmentation—the strategic, ambitious part of her personality pulling in one direction, her deeper ethical commitments pulling in another.

Her relationship with Gabriel became a complex terrain of support and challenging dialogue. Where once their conversations had been explorations of shared professional vision, they now became deep negotiations of ethical boundaries.

"You're carrying a burden that goes beyond professional decision-making," Gabriel observed during one particularly intense conversation. "This is about the kind of future you want to help create."

The personal cost was immediate and visceral. Sleepless nights gave way to intense periods of self-reflection. Her typically methodical approach to problem-solving seemed inadequate in the face of such profound ethical complexity.

Rosa Martinez—her longtime friend from the community center—provided a perspective rooted in lived experience.

"Technology isn't neutral," Rosa told her. "Every algorithm, every system we create carries the imprint of our values, our understanding of human potential."

The sacrifices became increasingly clear. Accepting the Nexus project might provide unprecedented professional resources, but it would require compromising certain fundamental beliefs about individual privacy and technological ethics.

Rejecting it would mean walking away from a level of research funding and institutional support she had spent years positioning herself to receive.

Her mother's wisdom resonated in these moments of profound uncertainty. "Sometimes," Maria Rodriguez would say, "survival isn't about taking every available path. Sometimes it's about choosing the path that allows you to remain true to yourself."

The emotional landscape became increasingly complex. Her ambition—that driving force that had propelled her from her immigrant neighborhood to the forefront of urban innovation research—now seemed to be in direct conflict with her deepest ethical commitments.

6.3 The Price of Progress

The internal conflict manifested in unexpected ways. Elena found her typically precise research methodology becoming increasingly introspective. Each dataset, each algorithmic model became not just a technical challenge, but a moral inquiry.

Her conversations with Marcus took on a philosophical depth that went far beyond their previous collaborative work.

"We're not just developing technologies," Marcus observed. "We're essentially creating new languages of human interaction. And languages, ultimately, shape how we understand ourselves and each other."

The psychological weight was substantial. Elena began to see her entire professional journey through a different lens—not as a linear progression of achievements, but as a complex negotiation between individual potential and broader social responsibilities.

Gabriel's perspective proved increasingly valuable. Where others might have seen her ethical deliberation as a professional obstacle, he recognized it as a profound form of intellectual and moral maturity.

"You're not just making a decision about a research project," he told her. "You're defining the boundaries of technological ethics."

The process of decision-making became a form of psychological exploration. Elena realized that her ambition was evolving—from a purely individual drive for achievement to a more complex understanding of professional responsibility.

Her research team watched this transformation with a mixture of respect and curiosity. They understood that something profound was happening—not just a professional decision, but a fundamental reimagining of their collective approach to technological innovation.

The Nexus project invitation remained, a constant reminder of the complex intersection between professional opportunity and ethical commitment.

As weeks turned into months, Elena's approach crystallized. The solution would not be a simple binary choice—accept or reject. Instead, she would use this opportunity to create a new framework for technological development.

She would propose a radical alternative: a research methodology that prioritized individual agency, that built privacy protections into the fundamental architecture of the technological systems.

"We're not just developing algorithms," she would later tell her team. "We're creating a new language of technological ethics."

The decision represented more than a professional strategy. It was a profound statement about the kind of future she believed was possible—a future where technological innovation and human dignity were not in conflict, but in dynamic, generative dialogue.

Her journey had always been about transformation. But now, that transformation extended far beyond individual achievement. It was about reimagining the very possibilities of technological progress.

The cost of ambition, Elena was learning, was not measured in professional sacrifices. It was measured in the depth of one's commitment to creating meaningful, ethical change.

And that, she was discovering, was the most profound form of progress imaginable.

Chapter 7: Psychological Warfare

7.1 Emotional Resilience

The aftermath of the Nexus Innovations decision reverberated through Elena Rodriguez's professional and personal landscape like a carefully calibrated seismic wave. Her choice to propose an alternative research framework—one that prioritized ethical considerations and individual agency—had not been without consequences.

In the weeks following her proposal, Elena discovered that true resilience was not about avoiding conflict, but about maintaining one's core integrity in the face of institutional pressure.

The academic review board's response was swift and multifaceted. Some viewed her approach as revolutionary, others as professionally naive. Colleagues who had once been supportive now maintained a calculated distance, their professional courtesies tinged with a subtle undertone of skepticism.

Her mother's voice echoed in these moments of professional isolation. "Resilience is not about being unbreakable," Maria Rodriguez would say. "It's about knowing how to reassemble yourself after being broken."

Gabriel became more than a romantic partner during this period—he became a strategic ally, helping Elena navigate the complex psychological terrain of professional challenge.

"They're testing your resolve," he observed during one of their late-night strategy sessions. "Every institution has its own immune system, designed to reject approaches that challenge existing paradigms."

Elena's approach was methodical. She began documenting every interaction, every subtle shift in professional dynamics. Her research methodology, which had always been about understanding complex systems, now turned inward—analyzing the intricate social ecosystems of academic and technological innovation.

Marcus, her longtime research collaborator, provided a crucial counterpoint. "Your resilience," he told her, "is not just about surviving this moment. It's about creating a new pathway for future researchers."

The psychological challenge was profound. Elena was simultaneously defending her professional approach and reimagining the very concepts of technological research and ethical innovation.

Her immigrant background became a source of unexpected strength. The Rodriguez family's history of survival—of navigating complex social landscapes with strategic intelligence—provided a foundational resilience that transcended individual professional challenges.

7.2 Manipulating Perceptions

Perception, Elena was learning, was as much a technological system as any algorithm she had ever designed. It could be analyzed, understood, and strategically navigated.

Her approach to the institutional pushback was not defensive, but strategically proactive. She began cultivating a network of allies—not through traditional networking, but through genuine intellectual engagement.

Young researchers, particularly those from marginalized backgrounds, began to see her as more than a professional figure. She became a strategic mentor, helping them understand that professional advancement was not just about individual achievement, but about creating broader systemic possibilities.

Rosa Martinez observed this transformation with a knowing smile. "You're not just managing perceptions," Rosa said. "You're creating an entirely new narrative of professional engagement."

The manipulation of perception was subtle and sophisticated. Elena didn't seek to convince her critics through confrontation, but through the consistent demonstration of a more holistic approach to technological innovation.

She began publishing a series of nuanced academic papers that didn't just critique existing research frameworks but offered comprehensive alternative methodologies. Each paper was a carefully constructed argument, blending technical precision with ethical consideration.

Gabriel's background in policy development proved invaluable. Together, they developed strategies that went beyond traditional academic discourse, creating interdisciplinary conversations that challenged existing institutional boundaries.

"You're rewriting the language of professional engagement," Gabriel told her. "Not by fighting the existing system, but by demonstrating the limitations of its current approach."

Her strategy involved multiple layers of social intelligence. She understood that perception was not about individual interactions, but about creating comprehensive ecosystems of understanding.

Young researchers began gravitating towards her approach. Where traditional academic mentorship had been hierarchical and competitive, Elena created collaborative networks that valued collective growth over individual achievement.

7.3 Psychological Survival Strategies

The psychological toll of sustained institutional pressure was substantial. Elena developed a complex set of coping mechanisms that went far beyond traditional stress management.

Meditation, which she had previously approached with academic skepticism, became a strategic tool of psychological recalibration. But her practice was not about passive relaxation—it was an active form of mental training, a way of developing psychological flexibility.

Her father's engineering background informed her approach. "Resilience," Carlos Rodriguez would say, "is about understanding systems—whether they're mechanical or psychological. It's about identifying pressure points, understanding flow, creating adaptive mechanisms."

Elena began documenting her psychological strategies with the same meticulous approach she applied to her research. She developed what she called a "psychological resilience framework"—a systematic approach to understanding and managing institutional and personal challenges.

The framework had multiple components:

1. **Emotional Mapping**: Systematically tracking emotional responses to professional challenges, identifying patterns and developing strategic interventions.
2. **Cognitive Reframing**: Transforming professional challenges from threats to opportunities for systemic understanding and personal growth.

3. **Strategic Network Development**: Creating supportive ecosystems that provide both emotional and professional sustenance.

Marcus was fascinated by her approach. "You're essentially developing a technological approach to psychological management," he observed. "Treating emotional resilience as a complex adaptive system."

Her conversations with Gabriel became profound explorations of psychological strategy. Where traditional approaches to stress management might focus on individual coping, their discussions centered on broader systemic understanding.

"Psychological survival," Gabriel would argue, "is not about individual endurance. It's about creating adaptive frameworks that transform challenge into opportunity."

The Rodriguez family's immigrant history became a profound source of psychological strategy. Generations of navigating complex social landscapes had created a deep reservoir of adaptive intelligence.

Rosa Martinez recognized this profound transformation. "You're not just surviving," she told Elena. "You're creating an entirely new approach to professional and personal resilience."

Elena's psychological survival strategies extended beyond individual coping. She began developing workshops and mentorship programs that taught young researchers—particularly those from marginalized backgrounds—how to navigate complex institutional landscapes.

Her approach was revolutionary. Instead of teaching traditional professional skills, she focused on developing comprehensive adaptive intelligence—the ability to understand, navigate, and ultimately transform complex social and professional systems.

The psychological warfare was not about conquest, but about continuous adaptation. Each challenge became an opportunity for deeper understanding, for more sophisticated approaches to professional and personal growth.

As the academic and technological landscapes continued to shift, Elena Rodriguez stood at the intersection of multiple complex systems—technological, social, psychological. Her resilience was not about remaining unchanged, but about developing the capacity for continuous, strategic transformation.

The true measure of psychological strength, she was learning, was not about resistance, but about the ability to reimagine possibilities in the face of sustained challenge.

And in that reimagining lay her most profound power.

Chapter 8: Intellectual Pursuits

8.1 Knowledge as Liberation

The small community center where Elena Rodriguez had spent countless hours of her youth now became an unexpected laboratory of intellectual transformation. What had once been a space of survival and community support was evolving into a radical center of educational innovation.

Her approach to knowledge was never about academic accumulation. It was about liberation—a concept deeply rooted in her family's immigrant experience, in the belief that understanding could be the most powerful form of personal and collective empowerment.

The program she developed was revolutionary in its simplicity and depth. Rather than traditional educational models that treated knowledge as a fixed commodity to be transferred, Elena conceptualized learning as a dynamic, collaborative process of discovery.

"Knowledge is not something you acquire," she would tell the diverse group of participants—young professionals, immigrant workers, community activists. "It's a conversation you enter, a landscape you continuously explore and reshape."

Her methodology drew from multiple disciplines. The precision of her technological background merged with the narrative richness of sociological understanding. Each educational module was carefully designed to not just impart information, but to develop comprehensive adaptive intelligence.

Rosa Martinez, who had been her mentor in the community center years ago, now stood beside her as a collaborator. "You're not just teaching," Rosa observed. "You're creating pathways of possibility."

The educational strategy had multiple innovative components:

1. **Contextual Learning**: Every technical concept was contextualized within broader social and personal narratives.
2. **Collaborative Knowledge Generation**: Participants were not passive recipients but active co-creators of understanding.
3. **Interdisciplinary Integration**: Boundaries between traditional academic disciplines were deliberately blurred, encouraging holistic

thinking.

Gabriel's background in policy development provided crucial insights. Together, they developed an approach that saw education as a form of social innovation—a method of creating broader systemic transformation.

"We're not just transferring skills," Gabriel would argue during their collaborative design sessions. "We're developing cognitive ecosystems that can adapt to complex, changing environments."

The community center became more than an educational space. It was a living laboratory of intellectual possibilities, a place where traditional barriers of access were systematically dismantled.

8.2 Challenging Intellectual Boundaries [Personal Growth]

Intellectual growth, for Elena, was never about individual achievement. It was about creating broader pathways of understanding, about challenging the very concept of intellectual boundaries.

Her research began to take on a more holistic dimension. Where her previous work had focused on technological systems, she now explored the intricate connections between technological innovation, social dynamics, and individual potential.

Marcus, her longtime research collaborator, recognized the profound shift. "You're developing a new language of understanding," he observed. "One that doesn't just describe systems, but reveals their interconnected potential."

The boundaries she challenged were both institutional and conceptual. Traditional academic frameworks that separated disciplines—technology from sociology, individual experience from collective understanding—were deliberately and systematically questioned.

A series of interdisciplinary symposiums became her primary platform. Researchers from technology, sociology, urban planning, and community development were brought together not as competitors, but as collaborative explorers.

Her approach was systematic yet profoundly creative. Each symposium was carefully designed to create moments of unexpected connection, to reveal the invisible threads that connected seemingly disparate fields of study.

"Intellectual boundaries," Elena would argue, "are often artificial constructs that limit our capacity to understand complex systems."

The personal growth was as significant as the intellectual exploration. Each challenge to existing frameworks became an opportunity for deeper self-understanding, for reimagining the very concept of knowledge.

Her immigrant background provided a unique perspective. The Rodriguez family's history of navigating complex social landscapes had always been about understanding systems, about seeing connections that others might miss.

8.3 The Power of Continuous Learning [Self-Improvement]

Continuous learning was not an academic concept for Elena, but a fundamental approach to existence. It was a dynamic process of constant adaptation, of seeing every experience as an opportunity for deeper understanding.

Her personal learning ecosystem was complex and multifaceted. Traditional academic research merged with community engagement, technological innovation intersected with social narrative, personal experience became a source of profound theoretical insight.

Gabriel's influence was significant. Their conversations became intellectual explorations that transcended traditional academic discourse. They didn't just discuss research—they reimagined the very concept of knowledge generation.

"Learning is not about accumulation," Gabriel would often say. "It's about continuous transformation."

Elena developed what she called a "adaptive learning framework"—a systematic approach to personal and collective intellectual growth. The framework had several key components:

1. **Reflective Practice**: Continuous critical examination of personal assumptions and intellectual frameworks.
2. **Collaborative Knowledge Generation**: Creating spaces where diverse perspectives could interact and generate new understanding.
3. **Systemic Thinking**: Understanding knowledge not as isolated facts, but as interconnected, dynamic systems.

Her mother Maria's wisdom echoed in this approach. "Knowledge is not something you possess," Maria would say. "It's something you're in constant dialogue with."

The learning was never solitary. Elena created networks of continuous intellectual exploration—online platforms, community workshops, interdisciplinary research groups that blurred the lines between academic institution and living laboratory.

Young researchers, particularly those from marginalized backgrounds, found in her approach a radical reimagining of intellectual possibility. She wasn't just offering educational opportunities—she was creating entire ecosystems of potential.

Rosa Martinez observed this transformation with profound appreciation. "You're not just learning," Rosa would tell her. "You're creating new languages of understanding."

The technological tools Elena developed were as innovative as her philosophical approach. Adaptive learning platforms that could recognize individual learning patterns, that could create personalized educational journeys based on complex algorithmic understanding.

But these were never about technological solution alone. They were always about human potential, about creating broader pathways of collective understanding.

Her research began to attract international attention. Academic institutions, technology companies, social innovation organizations—all recognized that Elena was developing something more than a new educational methodology. She was creating a comprehensive approach to human potential.

The boundaries between personal growth, technological innovation, and social transformation became increasingly fluid. Elena Rodriguez was not just a researcher or an educator. She was an architect of possibility, continuously reimagining the very concept of knowledge.

As the intellectual landscapes continued to shift, she stood at their complex intersection—not as an observer, but as a creative force of continuous transformation.

Knowledge, she was demonstrating, was never a destination. It was always a journey of endless, beautiful possibility.

Chapter 9: Romantic Rebellion

9.1 Defying Social Expectations

The Rodriguez family gatherings had always been a complex terrain of cultural expectations, unspoken rules, and intricate social negotiations. But the gathering where Elena introduced Gabriel marked a profound moment of romantic and personal rebellion.

Her extended family—a sprawling network of aunts, uncles, cousins, and distant relatives—represented a microcosm of immigrant social dynamics. Generations of careful social positioning, of strategic navigation through complex cultural landscapes, had created an intricate web of expectations.

Gabriel was not the partner they had anticipated. He was not simply a successful professional from a similar background. He was a collaborator, an intellectual equal who challenged every traditional notion of romantic partnership.

The family dinner became a carefully choreographed dance of cultural expectations and personal authenticity. Elena's mother, Maria, watched with a mixture of curiosity and strategic observation. Her father, Carlos, approached the interaction with his characteristic engineering precision.

"He's not just your partner," Carlos observed quietly to Elena during a moment of private conversation. "He's your collaborative partner in reimagining possibility."

The contrast was deliberate and profound. Where traditional romantic narratives suggested a clear division between personal and professional domains, Elena and Gabriel represented a radical integration. Their relationship was not about traditional romantic ideals, but about creating a comprehensive partnership of intellectual and emotional potential.

Rosa Martinez, Elena's longtime friend and mentor, recognized the deeper significance. "You're not just challenging romantic conventions," Rosa told her. "You're reimagining the entire concept of partnership."

Gabriel's approach was equally strategic. He didn't seek to replace or diminish Elena's family dynamics but to engage with them as a complex social ecosystem to be understood and navigated.

His conversations with Elena's family were never about proving himself. They were about creating genuine connections, about understanding the complex narratives that had shaped their experiences.

The Rodriguez family's immigrant background became a crucial context. Generations of strategic survival, of carefully negotiating social landscapes, had created a sophisticated understanding of social dynamics.

Elena understood that her romantic rebellion was not about rejection, but about expansion—about creating broader possibilities of connection and understanding.

9.2 Passion Against Convention

The passion between Elena and Gabriel transcended traditional romantic narratives. It was a collaborative exploration of personal and intellectual potential, a continuous dialogue of mutual growth and challenge.

Their relationship became a living laboratory of personal freedom. Where conventional romantic frameworks suggested compromise and reduction, they created a partnership of expansion and mutual empowerment.

Gabriel's background in policy development and Elena's technological research created a unique intellectual synergy. Their conversations were never about winning arguments but about generating new understanding, about creating comprehensive perspectives that neither could have developed individually.

"We're not just partners," Gabriel would often say. "We're collaborative architects of possibility."

The personal freedom they created was multilayered. It wasn't about rejecting traditional relationship structures but about deliberately constructing a partnership that honored individual potential.

Their approach to personal space was revolutionary. Neither sought to constrain or define the other. Instead, they created a dynamic ecosystem of mutual support and challenge.

Marcus, Elena's research collaborator, observed this unique dynamic with fascination. "You've transformed the very concept of partnership," he told them. "It's not about completion. It's about continuous collaborative evolution."

The freedom they created was not about individual independence, but about interdependent growth. Each challenge became an opportunity for deeper understanding, each conflict a pathway to more sophisticated connection.

Elena's mother, Maria, recognized the profound nature of their relationship. "True partnership," she would tell Elena, "is not about finding someone who makes you whole. It's about finding someone who helps you continuously reimagine your potential."

Their romantic rebellion was subtle yet profound. They didn't fight against existing relationship models. They simply created something so fundamentally different that traditional frameworks became irrelevant.

9.3 Love as Revolutionary Act

Love, in Elena and Gabriel's conceptualization, was never a passive experience. It was an active, creative force—a continuous process of mutual transformation and collective potential generation.

Their emotional connection became a form of social innovation. They saw their relationship not as a private domain separate from their professional and social worlds, but as a comprehensive ecosystem of possibility.

The revolutionary aspect was in their approach. Emotional vulnerability was not seen as weakness but as a sophisticated form of strategic engagement. Each moment of genuine connection became an opportunity for deeper understanding.

Gabriel's approach to emotional intelligence was as strategic as Elena's technological research. "Emotions are complex adaptive systems," he would argue during their philosophical discussions. "They're not fixed states, but dynamic landscapes of potential."

Their collaborative work began to reflect this holistic approach. Research projects that might have been traditionally segregated—technological innovation, social policy, emotional intelligence—became integrated explorations of human potential.

Rosa Martinez observed this transformation with profound appreciation. "You're creating a new language of emotional engagement," she told them. "One that sees love as a creative, transformative force."

The emotional empowerment they generated extended beyond their personal relationship. They created mentorship programs, collaborative research initiatives that saw emotional intelligence as a crucial form of social and professional capability.

Elena's technological research began to incorporate more nuanced understandings of human emotional complexity. Algorithms were no longer just about data processing but about understanding complex emotional ecosystems.

Their love became a form of social resistance. Not through confrontation, but through the continuous demonstration of a more expansive, integrated approach to human potential.

The Rodriguez family's immigrant background provided a crucial context. Generations of survival had required sophisticated emotional intelligence, a deep understanding of social navigation.

"Emotional power," Carlos Rodriguez would say, reflecting on their approach, "is about understanding complex systems. Not just external social landscapes, but the intricate internal ecosystems of human experience."

As their relationship continued to evolve, Elena and Gabriel became more than romantic partners. They were collaborative architects of a new understanding of human connection—one that saw love not as a private emotional refuge, but as a profound force of social and personal transformation.

Their rebellion was not loud or confrontational. It was a continuous, subtle reimagining of possibility—a demonstration that love could be a comprehensive, creative act of mutual empowerment.

In a world of rigid social expectations and limited romantic narratives, they were creating something radical: a partnership of continuous, collaborative becoming.

Love, they were showing, was not about finding someone who completed you. It was about finding someone who helped you continuously reimagine your own potential.

Chapter 10: Economic Maneuvering

10.1 Financial Strategy

The Rodriguez family's economic history was etched into Elena's understanding of financial survival—a complex narrative of strategic navigation, resilience, and continuous adaptation.

Her father's engineering manuals, carefully preserved and annotated, had been more than technical documents. They were maps of economic possibility, testament to the immigrant experience of transforming limited resources into sustainable opportunities.

The startup incubator Elena established was not just a professional initiative. It was a comprehensive economic strategy, a deliberate attempt to create systemic pathways for economic mobility, particularly for researchers and innovators from marginalized backgrounds.

Her approach was methodical and revolutionary. Traditional startup funding models prioritized quick returns and easily marketable technologies. Elena's model was fundamentally different—it valued long-term potential, social impact, and innovative approaches that challenged existing economic paradigms.

Carlos Rodriguez's lessons echoed in every strategic decision. "Economic survival," he would say, spreading out complex engineering schematics on their small apartment's dining table, "is about understanding systems, not just accumulating resources."

The incubator became a living laboratory of economic innovation. Each project was carefully evaluated not just on potential financial returns, but on its capacity to create broader systemic transformation.

Gabriel's background in policy development provided crucial insights. Together, they developed a funding model that integrated social impact metrics, technological potential, and comprehensive economic analysis.

"We're not just funding startups," Gabriel would argue during their strategic planning sessions. "We're creating ecosystems of economic possibility."

10.2 Wealth as Social Currency

Wealth, in Elena's conceptualization, was never about individual accumulation. It was a complex form of social capital, a dynamic resource that could be strategically deployed to create broader systemic opportunities.

Her approach challenged traditional economic frameworks. Where conventional models saw wealth as a personal achievement, Elena saw it as a collaborative potential—a resource to be strategically distributed and leveraged for collective advancement.

The network she developed was extraordinary. Young researchers, technological innovators, community activists—all became part of a comprehensive economic ecosystem that transcended traditional funding models.

Rosa Martinez, who had been her mentor in the community center, recognized the profound nature of this approach. "You're not just redistributing resources," Rosa observed. "You're reimagining the entire concept of economic potential."

Each investment was a carefully calculated strategic move. Elena didn't just provide funding. She created comprehensive support systems—mentorship networks, collaborative research platforms, strategic connection opportunities.

Her technological background informed her economic strategy. Just as she approached technological systems as complex, adaptive ecosystems, she saw economic resources as dynamic, interconnected networks of potential.

The Rodriguez family's immigrant experience provided a crucial contextual framework. Generations of strategic survival had required a sophisticated understanding of economic navigation—of transforming limited resources into sustainable opportunities.

"Economic positioning," Carlos would tell her, "is about understanding the invisible infrastructures of opportunity."

The wealth Elena generated was never about personal accumulation. It was a strategic tool for creating broader systemic transformation, for developing comprehensive pathways of economic mobility.

10.3 Navigating Economic Landscapes

Financial intelligence, for Elena, was a complex, multidimensional skill. It wasn't about predictive algorithms or traditional economic modeling. It was about developing a comprehensive understanding of economic ecosystems, of seeing the intricate connections between technological innovation, social dynamics, and economic potential.

Her approach integrated multiple disciplines. Technological research merged with sociological understanding, economic analysis became a collaborative exploration of human potential.

The economic platforms she developed were revolutionary. They didn't just provide funding or resources. They created comprehensive ecosystems of economic possibility—platforms that could recognize and nurture innovative potential across diverse social and technological landscapes.

Gabriel's policy development background provided crucial strategic insights. Together, they developed economic models that saw financial resources as dynamic, adaptive systems rather than static accumulations.

"Economic navigation," Gabriel would argue, "is about understanding complex, interconnected landscapes of possibility."

Elena's technological background allowed her to develop sophisticated algorithmic approaches to economic analysis. But these were never just about data processing. They were about creating more nuanced, adaptive understanding of economic potential.

The platforms she developed could identify innovative potential in ways traditional economic models missed. They didn't just look at traditional metrics like educational background or existing resources. They developed comprehensive assessment frameworks that could recognize potential across diverse social and technological landscapes.

Rosa Martinez observed this transformation with profound appreciation. "You're not just analyzing economic potential," Rosa would tell her. "You're creating new languages of economic understanding."

The economic landscapes Elena navigated were complex and multilayered. She wasn't just operating within existing economic frameworks. She was deliberately creating new pathways of economic possibility.

Her immigrant background provided a crucial perspective. The Rodriguez family's experience of economic survival had always been about strategic navigation, about seeing opportunities in complex, challenging environments.

"Economic intelligence," Carlos would say, reflecting on their family's journey, "is about seeing potential where others see limitation."

The technology platforms Elena developed were extraordinary. They could analyze economic potential across complex, intersectional landscapes—recognizing innovative potential in ways that transcended traditional economic metrics.

Machine learning algorithms merged with sociological analysis, creating comprehensive economic assessment frameworks that could identify potential across diverse social and technological landscapes.

But these were never just about technological solutions. They were always about human potential, about creating broader pathways of economic mobility and innovative possibility.

As economic landscapes continued to shift and transform, Elena Rodriguez stood at their complex intersection—not as an observer, but as a creative force of continuous economic reimagination.

Her approach was fundamentally revolutionary. Economic strategy was not about individual achievement or resource accumulation. It was about creating comprehensive ecosystems of opportunity, about developing broader pathways of collective potential.

Wealth, she was demonstrating, was never just about money. It was about creating systematic pathways of human transformation.

And in that transformation lay her most profound economic innovation.

Chapter 11: Psychological Transformation

11.1 Breaking Internal Barriers

The mirror in Elena Rodriguez's home office reflected more than her physical image. It was a window into the complex psychological landscape she had spent years carefully navigating, challenging, and ultimately transforming.

Her internal barriers were not simple obstacles to be overcome. They were intricate psychological constructs—layers of inherited expectations, familial narratives, and societal limitations that had shaped her understanding of personal potential.

The Rodriguez family's immigrant experience had been her first lesson in psychological navigation. Survival had required more than physical resilience. It demanded a sophisticated psychological flexibility, an ability to reimagine possibility in the face of systemic constraints.

Her father, Carlos, had been her first teacher of psychological strategy. "Limitations," he would say, spreading out complex engineering schematics, "are often just poorly understood systems waiting to be redesigned."

The psychological work was methodical and profound. Elena began documenting her internal landscapes with the same precision she applied to her technological research. Each memory, each inherited belief became a data point in a comprehensive process of psychological deconstruction.

Gabriel's approach to psychological exploration complemented her analytical methodology. Where she approached internal barriers with technological precision, he brought a nuanced understanding of emotional complexity.

"Psychological barriers," Gabriel would observe during their deep conversations, "are not walls to be torn down. They're complex adaptive systems to be understood and reimagined."

The process was never about rejection. It was about understanding—about seeing the intricate ways that familial narratives, cultural expectations, and personal experiences had shaped her internal landscape.

Rosa Martinez, her longtime mentor, recognized the profound nature of this transformation. "You're not just breaking barriers," Rosa told her. "You're creating entirely new languages of personal potential."

11.2 Reimagining Personal Identity

Personal identity, for Elena, was never a fixed construct. It was a dynamic, continuously evolving ecosystem of potential—a complex interaction between inherited narratives, personal experiences, and intentional reimagination.

The transformation was multilayered. Her technological research began to merge with her personal psychological exploration. She saw identity not as a static entity, but as a sophisticated adaptive system—capable of continuous recalibration and growth.

Her work developed a revolutionary framework of personal identity. Traditional psychological models saw identity as a relatively stable construct. Elena's approach was fundamentally different—identity as a continuous process of creative reimagination.

Marcus, her longtime research collaborator, was fascinated by her approach. "You're developing a technological understanding of personal transformation," he observed. "Not just describing identity, but creating frameworks for intentional psychological evolution."

The Rodriguez family's immigrant background provided a crucial contextual framework. Generations of survival had required a sophisticated ability to adapt, to reimagine personal potential in complex, challenging environments.

Elena developed what she called an "identity adaptation framework"—a comprehensive approach to understanding personal transformation. The framework had multiple sophisticated components:

1. **Narrative Deconstruction**: Systematically examining inherited personal and familial narratives
2. **Adaptive Identity Modeling**: Creating flexible psychological frameworks
3. **Intentional Personal Evolution**: Developing strategies for continuous self-reimagination

Her conversations with Gabriel became profound explorations of personal potential. They didn't just discuss personal growth. They created comprehensive models of psychological transformation.

"Identity," Gabriel would argue, "is not something you are. It's something you continuously create."

The technological tools Elena developed were extraordinary. Adaptive psychological assessment platforms that could recognize complex patterns of personal limitation and potential, that could create personalized transformation strategies.

But these were never just about technological solution. They were always about human potential, about creating broader pathways of personal psychological liberation.

11.3 The Evolution of Self

The evolution of self was not a linear journey for Elena. It was a complex, multidimensional process of continuous reimagination—a profound metamorphosis that challenged every traditional understanding of personal growth.

Her technological background provided a unique lens. She approached personal transformation with the same systematic curiosity she applied to complex technological systems. Each psychological pattern was a dataset, each limitation a system waiting to be understood and redesigned.

The metamorphosis was comprehensive. It wasn't just about personal achievement or individual growth. It was about creating entirely new languages of human potential—about demonstrating that personal transformation could be a deliberate, strategic process.

Rosa Martinez observed this transformation with profound appreciation. "You're not just changing," Rosa would tell her. "You're creating entire new ecosystems of personal possibility."

Elena's work began to attract international attention. Psychological researchers, technological innovators, social transformation experts—all recognized that she was developing something more than a personal transformation methodology. She was creating a comprehensive approach to human potential.

The boundaries between personal growth, technological innovation, and psychological understanding became increasingly fluid. Elena Rodriguez was not just a researcher or a technologist. She was an architect of psychological possibility, continuously reimagining the very concept of human potential.

Her mother's wisdom echoed in these moments of profound transformation. "True growth," Maria Rodriguez would say, "is not about becoming something fixed. It's about developing the capacity for continuous becoming."

The technological platforms Elena developed were extraordinary. Machine learning algorithms merged with psychological analysis, creating comprehensive personal transformation frameworks that could recognize potential across complex, intersectional psychological landscapes.

But these were never just about technological solutions. They were always about human potential, about creating broader pathways of psychological liberation and creative reimagination.

Her personal metamorphosis became a form of social innovation. She didn't just transform herself. She created frameworks that could help others recognize and develop their own potential for continuous psychological evolution.

The Rodriguez family's immigrant background provided a crucial context. Generations of survival had required a sophisticated ability to adapt, to reimagine personal potential in complex, challenging environments.

"Transformation," Carlos would reflect, "is about developing the capacity to see possibility where others see limitations."

As psychological landscapes continued to shift and transform, Elena Rodriguez stood at their complex intersection—not as an observer, but as a creative force of continuous personal reimagination.

Her approach was fundamentally revolutionary. Personal growth was not about achieving a fixed state of development. It was about creating comprehensive ecosystems of psychological possibility, about developing broader pathways of continuous human potential.

Identity, she was demonstrating, was never a destination. It was always a journey of endless, beautiful becoming.

Chapter 12: Social Negotiations

12.1 Mastering Social Dynamics

The art of social navigation was never about manipulation for Elena Rodriguez. It was a sophisticated ecosystem of understanding—a complex interplay of perception, strategy, and genuine human connection.

Her approach to social dynamics emerged from the intricate landscape of her immigrant family's experiences. The Rodriguez family had survived not through confrontation, but through a nuanced understanding of social systems—reading unspoken narratives, anticipating institutional responses, and creating pathways where none seemed to exist.

Gabriel, her longtime intellectual companion, often observed the extraordinary complexity of her social intelligence. "You don't just interact with social systems," he would say. "You interpret them like elaborate technological networks—understanding their underlying logic, their hidden connections."

The social landscape was never a fixed terrain for Elena. It was a dynamic, continuously shifting environment that required constant recalibration. Her technological background provided her with a unique lens—each social interaction became a dataset, each relationship a complex system waiting to be understood and strategically navigated.

Her mentor Rosa Martinez had been instrumental in developing this sophisticated approach. "Social intelligence," Rosa would explain, "is about seeing beyond the immediate interaction. It's about understanding the deeper systemic narratives that shape human connections."

Elena's social strategy was multilayered. She didn't seek to dominate social spaces. Instead, she sought to understand them—to create meaningful connections that transcended traditional power dynamics. Her immigrant background had taught her that true social power wasn't about force, but about adaptive intelligence.

The psychological tools she developed weren't just theoretical constructs. They were practical frameworks for understanding complex social interactions. Machine learning algorithms merged with deep psychological insights, creating platforms that could analyze intricate social dynamics with unprecedented precision.

"Social navigation," she would tell her research team, "is about developing a comprehensive understanding of human complexity. It's not about winning. It's about creating meaningful, transformative connections."

12.2 Strategic Relationship Building

Relationship building for Elena was never a transactional process. It was a profound art of genuine connection—a delicate balance between strategic positioning and authentic human engagement.

Her networking approach emerged from her family's immigrant survival strategies. Carlos Rodriguez had always emphasized that meaningful connections were built on mutual understanding, not superficial exchanges. "A true network," he would say, "is an ecosystem of shared potential, not a collection of professional contacts."

The technological platforms Elena developed reflected this nuanced understanding. Her adaptive networking systems didn't just track professional connections. They mapped complex relational ecosystems—recognizing the intricate ways human relationships intersected with broader social and professional landscapes.

Marcus, her longtime research collaborator, was fascinated by her approach. "You're not just building a network," he observed. "You're creating intricate relational architectures that transform how people understand connection."

Elena's networking strategies were comprehensive:

1. **Relational Intelligence**: Deep understanding of individual motivations and systemic constraints
2. **Adaptive Connection Mapping**: Recognizing non-linear pathways of professional and personal influence
3. **Transformative Engagement**: Creating connections that expanded collective potential

Her conversations with Gabriel became profound explorations of relationship dynamics. They didn't just discuss networking strategies. They developed comprehensive models of human connection that challenged traditional understanding.

"Networking," Gabriel would argue, "is not about accumulating contacts. It's about creating ecosystems of mutual transformation."

The Rodriguez family's immigrant background provided a crucial contextual framework. Generations of survival had required a sophisticated ability to build strategic relationships across complex social boundaries—to create pathways of opportunity where systemic constraints seemed insurmountable.

Each relationship became a potential site of mutual growth. Elena didn't see networking as a zero-sum game, but as a complex, collaborative process of collective potential expansion.

Her international reputation grew not through aggressive self-promotion, but through a revolutionary approach to human connection. Researchers, technologists, and social transformation experts recognized that she was developing something far more profound than traditional networking strategies.

12.3 Navigating Complex Social Hierarchies

Social hierarchies were never simple vertical structures for Elena Rodriguez. They were sophisticated, multilayered ecosystems of power, perception, and potential—intricate networks waiting to be understood and strategically reimagined.

Her approach emerged from generations of immigrant experience—a deep understanding that social hierarchies were never fixed, but continuously negotiable landscapes of human potential. The Rodriguez family had survived by developing an extraordinary capacity to read, interpret, and strategically navigate complex social systems.

Rosa Martinez recognized the profound nature of Elena's social intelligence. "You're not just understanding social hierarchies," Rosa would tell her. "You're creating entirely new languages of institutional possibility."

The technological platforms Elena developed were extraordinary. Machine learning algorithms merged with deep sociological analysis, creating comprehensive frameworks that could recognize potential across complex, intersectional social landscapes.

Her social navigation strategies were never about simple rebellion or confrontation. They were about creating broader pathways of institutional transformation—demonstrating that social hierarchies could be sites of collective reimagination.

"Social intelligence," Elena would explain to her research team, "is about developing the capacity to see possibilities where others see limitations. It's about recognizing the fluid, adaptive nature of institutional power."

The boundaries between personal growth, technological innovation, and social understanding became increasingly fluid. Elena Rodriguez was not just a researcher or a technologist. She was an architect of social possibility, continuously reimagining the very concept of institutional potential.

Her mother's wisdom echoed in these moments of profound social analysis. "True social navigation," Maria Rodriguez would say, "is about developing the capacity to create connection where others see only division."

Elena's work began to attract international attention. Social researchers, technological innovators, transformation experts—all recognized that she was developing something more than a social navigation methodology. She was creating a comprehensive approach to understanding human potential within complex institutional landscapes.

The platforms she developed were never just about technological solutions. They were always about human potential, about creating broader pathways of social liberation and collective reimagination.

Her personal journey of social navigation became a form of broader social innovation. She didn't just transform her own understanding of institutional dynamics. She created frameworks that could help others recognize and develop their capacity for strategic social engagement.

"Navigation," Carlos would reflect, "is about developing the capacity to see connection where others see only separation."

As social landscapes continued to shift and transform, Elena Rodriguez stood at their complex intersection—not as an observer, but as a creative force of continuous social reimagination.

Her approach was fundamentally revolutionary. Social navigation was not about achieving a fixed position within existing hierarchies. It was about creating comprehensive ecosystems of collective potential, about developing broader pathways of human connection and institutional transformation.

Social intelligence, she was demonstrating, was never a destination. It was always a journey of endless, beautiful becoming—a continuous process of creating more expansive, more compassionate ways of understanding human potential.

Chapter 13: Emotional Resilience

13.1 Overcoming Personal Limitations

The mirror in Elena Rodriguez's study reflected more than her physical presence. It captured the intricate landscape of emotional resilience—a complex terrain she had meticulously cultivated through years of intentional psychological exploration.

Inner strength was never a singular construct for Elena. It was a sophisticated, multilayered ecosystem of emotional intelligence, adaptive capacity, and profound self-understanding. Each challenge, each moment of potential breakdown, became an opportunity for deeper psychological integration.

Her father, Carlos, had been her first teacher of emotional strategy. "Limitations," he would tell her, his engineering schematics spread across the kitchen table, "are often just unexplored territories of personal potential."

The Rodriguez family's immigrant experience had been a crucible of emotional endurance. Survival had demanded more than physical resilience—it required a nuanced emotional flexibility, an ability to transform potential suffering into profound personal growth.

Gabriel, her longtime intellectual companion, recognized the extraordinary depth of her emotional navigation. "You don't just overcome challenges," he would observe during their deep conversations. "You systematically deconstruct them, understanding their fundamental psychological architecture."

Elena's approach to inner strength was methodical and profound. She began documenting her emotional landscapes with the same precision she applied to her technological research. Each emotional challenge became a data point in a comprehensive process of psychological reconstruction.

Her research platforms developed sophisticated emotional resilience frameworks—machine learning algorithms that could map complex emotional patterns, identifying not just moments of vulnerability, but pathways of potential transformation.

"Inner strength," she would tell her research team, "is not about eliminating vulnerability. It's about developing a comprehensive capacity for emotional adaptation."

Rosa Martinez, her longtime mentor, saw something extraordinary in Elena's approach. "You're creating entirely new languages of emotional survival," Rosa would say, her eyes reflecting a deep understanding of psychological complexity.

The emotional work was never about suppression. It was about understanding—about seeing the intricate ways that familial narratives, cultural experiences, and personal challenges had shaped her emotional landscape.

13.2 Psychological Endurance

Emotional survival for Elena was a dynamic, continuously evolving process—a sophisticated journey of psychological adaptation that went far beyond traditional understanding of resilience.

Her technological background provided a unique lens. She approached emotional challenges with the same systematic curiosity she applied to complex technological systems. Each psychological pattern was a dataset, each emotional challenge a system waiting to be understood and redesigned.

The Rodriguez family's immigrant background provided a crucial contextual framework. Generations of survival had required a sophisticated ability to adapt, to reimagine emotional potential in complex, challenging environments.

Marcus, her research collaborator, was fascinated by her approach. "You're developing a technological understanding of emotional endurance," he observed. "Not just describing survival, but creating frameworks for intentional emotional evolution."

Elena developed what she called an "emotional adaptation framework"—a comprehensive approach to understanding psychological survival. The framework had multiple sophisticated components:

1. **Emotional Deconstruction**: Systematically examining inherited emotional narratives
2. **Adaptive Resilience Modeling**: Creating flexible psychological

response mechanisms
3. **Intentional Emotional Evolution**: Developing strategies for continuous emotional growth

Her conversations with Gabriel became profound explorations of psychological endurance. They didn't just discuss emotional survival. They created comprehensive models of how human beings could transform potential psychological limitations into sources of strength.

"Emotional survival," Gabriel would argue, "is not about resistance. It's about developing a comprehensive capacity for continuous psychological reimagination."

The technological tools Elena developed were extraordinary. Adaptive psychological assessment platforms that could recognize complex patterns of emotional limitation and potential, that could create personalized resilience strategies.

But these were never just about technological solutions. They were always about human potential, about creating broader pathways of emotional liberation and psychological adaptation.

Her work began to attract international attention. Psychological researchers, technological innovators, social transformation experts—all recognized that she was developing something more than an emotional survival methodology. She was creating a comprehensive approach to human psychological potential.

13.3 The Power of Emotional Adaptation

The power of emotional adaptation was never about eliminating challenges for Elena Rodriguez. It was about developing a profound capacity to transform potential suffering into sources of unprecedented personal growth.

Her approach to resilience was fundamentally revolutionary. Traditional psychological models saw emotional adaptation as a reactive process. Elena's framework was dynamic and intentional—a continuous process of psychological reimagination.

The technological platforms she developed merged sophisticated machine learning algorithms with deep psychological insights. These weren't just assessment tools. They were comprehensive ecosystems of emotional potential—platforms that could recognize complex emotional patterns and create personalized transformation strategies.

"Resilience," she would explain to her research team, "is about developing the capacity to see possibility where others see only limitation."

Her mother Maria's wisdom echoed in these moments of profound emotional exploration. "True adaptation," Maria would say, "is not about becoming invulnerable. It's about developing the capacity for continuous becoming."

The Rodriguez family's immigrant experience provided a crucial narrative of emotional resilience. Generations had survived not through resistance, but through a sophisticated ability to reimagine possibility in the face of complex challenges.

Rosa Martinez observed this transformation with profound appreciation. "You're not just developing resilience strategies," Rosa would tell her. "You're creating entire new ecosystems of emotional possibility."

Elena's work challenged every traditional understanding of emotional survival. She demonstrated that resilience was not a fixed state, but a continuous process of psychological evolution. Each emotional challenge became an opportunity for deeper understanding, for more sophisticated psychological integration.

The boundaries between personal growth, technological innovation, and emotional understanding became increasingly fluid. Elena Rodriguez was not just a researcher or a technologist. She was an architect of emotional possibility, continuously reimagining the very concept of human psychological potential.

Her platforms were never just about technological solutions. They were always about human potential, about creating broader pathways of emotional liberation and creative reimagination.

As psychological landscapes continued to shift and transform, Elena Rodriguez stood at their complex intersection—not as an observer, but as a creative force of continuous emotional adaptation.

Her approach was fundamentally revolutionary. Emotional resilience was not about achieving a fixed state of psychological stability. It was about creating comprehensive ecosystems of emotional possibility, about developing broader pathways of continuous human potential.

Resilience, she was demonstrating, was never a destination. It was always a journey of endless, beautiful becoming—a continuous process of creating more expansive, more compassionate ways of understanding human emotional potential.

Chapter 14: Romantic Complexity

14.1 Navigating Emotional Landscapes

The geography of love was never a simple terrain for Elena Rodriguez. It was an intricate, multidimensional landscape—a complex ecosystem of emotions, expectations, and profound human connections that defied traditional understanding.

Her approach to romantic relationships emerged from the same sophisticated analytical framework she applied to her technological and psychological research. Love was not a passive experience, but an active, intentional process of emotional exploration and mutual transformation.

Gabriel, her intellectual companion and most profound emotional collaborator, understood the depth of her romantic perspective. "You don't just experience relationships," he would observe. "You map them with the same precision you apply to complex technological systems."

The Rodriguez family's understanding of love had always been nuanced. Carlos and Maria Rodriguez had demonstrated a partnership that transcended romantic cliches—a deep collaboration of mutual respect, intellectual synergy, and continuous emotional growth.

Elena's technological platforms began to develop sophisticated relationship mapping tools. These were not simple dating algorithms or compatibility metrics. They were comprehensive ecosystems of emotional intelligence—platforms that could recognize the intricate dynamics of human connection.

"Romantic navigation," she would explain to her research team, "is about developing a comprehensive understanding of emotional ecosystems. It's about recognizing the profound potential for mutual transformation that exists within intimate connections."

Rosa Martinez, her longtime mentor, saw something extraordinary in Elena's approach to love. "You're creating entirely new languages of romantic possibility," Rosa would tell her, her eyes reflecting a deep understanding of emotional complexity.

Each romantic encounter became a site of profound research. Not in a clinical, detached sense, but as a genuine exploration of human potential. Elena understood that love was never about possession or limitation. It was about creating expansive spaces of mutual growth and understanding.

Her work challenged traditional notions of romantic relationships. Love was not a fixed state to be achieved, but a continuous process of emotional and intellectual co-creation.

14.2 Navigating Intimate Connections

Intimate connections for Elena were never simple linear experiences. They were sophisticated, multilayered ecosystems of emotional and intellectual exchange—complex networks of potential transformation.

Her technological background provided a unique lens for understanding romantic complexity. She approached relationships with the same systematic curiosity she applied to complex technological systems. Each emotional interaction became a dataset, each moment of connection a system waiting to be understood and reimagined.

Marcus, her research collaborator, was fascinated by her approach. "You're developing a technological understanding of romantic dynamics," he observed. "Not just describing relationships, but creating frameworks for intentional emotional evolution."

Elena developed what she called an "intimate connection framework"—a comprehensive approach to understanding the profound complexity of romantic relationships. The framework had multiple sophisticated components:

1. **Emotional Topology**: Mapping the intricate emotional landscapes of intimate connections
2. **Adaptive Relationship Modeling**: Creating flexible frameworks for mutual growth
3. **Transformative Intimacy Strategies**: Developing approaches to continuous relational evolution

Her conversations with Gabriel became profound explorations of romantic complexity. They didn't just discuss relationships. They created comprehensive models of how human beings could transform intimate connections into sites of mutual psychological and intellectual growth.

"Romantic complexity," Gabriel would argue, "is about recognizing the extraordinary potential for mutual transformation that exists within genuine human connection."

The technological tools Elena developed were extraordinary. Adaptive relationship assessment platforms that could recognize complex patterns of emotional limitation and potential, that could create personalized strategies for deepening intimate understanding.

But these were never just about technological solutions. They were always about human potential, about creating broader pathways of emotional liberation and relational depth.

Her work began to attract international attention. Psychological researchers, relationship experts, and social transformation specialists all recognized that she was developing something far more profound than traditional relationship methodologies. She was creating a comprehensive approach to understanding human intimate potential.

The Rodriguez family's immigrant background provided a crucial contextual framework. Generations had navigated complex emotional landscapes, understanding that true intimacy was about mutual survival, intellectual synergy, and continuous emotional adaptation.

14.3 Love as a Source of Wisdom

Love, for Elena Rodriguez, was never a passive experience of emotional consumption. It was an active, intentional process of profound emotional and intellectual learning—a continuous journey of mutual transformation and deep human understanding.

Her approach to love challenged every traditional romantic narrative. Where popular culture presented love as a fixed state of emotional resolution, Elena saw it as a dynamic ecosystem of continuous growth, a sophisticated space of mutual psychological exploration.

The technological platforms she developed merged sophisticated machine learning algorithms with deep psychological insights. These weren't just relationship assessment tools. They were comprehensive ecosystems of emotional potential—platforms that could recognize complex relational patterns and create personalized transformation strategies.

"Love," she would explain to her research team, "is about developing the capacity to see profound human potential where others see only surface-level emotional exchange."

Her mother Maria's wisdom echoed in these moments of profound romantic exploration. "True intimacy," Maria would say, "is not about finding completion. It's about creating space for continuous mutual becoming."

Rosa Martinez observed this transformation with profound appreciation. "You're not just understanding romantic connections," Rosa would tell her. "You're creating entire new ecosystems of emotional and intellectual possibility."

Elena's work demonstrated that love was a sophisticated form of knowledge production. Each intimate connection became an opportunity for deeper understanding, for more nuanced psychological and intellectual integration.

The boundaries between personal growth, technological innovation, and emotional understanding became increasingly fluid. Elena Rodriguez was not just a researcher or a technologist. She was an architect of romantic possibility, continuously reimagining the very concept of human intimate potential.

Her platforms were never just about technological solutions. They were always about human potential, about creating broader pathways of emotional liberation and creative reimagination.

As romantic landscapes continued to shift and transform, Elena Rodriguez stood at their complex intersection—not as an observer, but as a creative force of continuous emotional and intellectual exploration.

Her approach was fundamentally revolutionary. Romantic complexity was not about achieving a fixed state of emotional resolution. It was about creating comprehensive ecosystems of intimate possibility, about developing broader pathways of continuous human potential.

Love, she was demonstrating, was never a destination. It was always a journey of endless, beautiful becoming—a continuous process of creating more expansive, more compassionate ways of understanding human emotional and intellectual potential.

In the intricate dance of intimate connection, Elena Rodriguez had discovered something profound: that love, in its most sophisticated form, was not about finding the perfect partner. It was about becoming the most authentic, most expensive version of oneself—and creating space for another to do the same.

Chapter 15: Professional Aspirations

15.1 Career Strategies

The trajectory of Elena Rodriguez's professional journey was never a linear path. It was a complex, multidimensional landscape of strategic innovation, continuous learning, and profound systemic transformation.

Her approach to career development emerged from the intricate survival strategies of her immigrant family—a sophisticated understanding that professional success was never about individual achievement, but about creating broader pathways of collective potential.

Carlos Rodriguez had been her first mentor of professional strategy. "A career," he would say, spreading out complex engineering schematics across their modest kitchen table, "is not a ladder to be climbed. It's an ecosystem to be cultivated."

The technological platforms Elena developed were extraordinary manifestations of this philosophy. They weren't simply career assessment tools. They were comprehensive ecosystems of professional potential—adaptive systems that could recognize complex professional landscapes and create personalized development strategies.

Gabriel, her intellectual companion, recognized the profound depth of her professional approach. "You don't just navigate career trajectories," he would observe during their deep conversations. "You systematically deconstruct and reimagine entire professional ecosystems."

Elena's career strategy was methodical and revolutionary:

1. **Systemic Professional Analysis**: Understanding institutional landscapes beyond traditional career frameworks
2. **Adaptive Skill Mapping**: Developing flexible professional capabilities
3. **Transformative Career Positioning**: Creating strategies that expanded collective professional potential

Rosa Martinez, her longtime mentor, saw something extraordinary in Elena's approach. "You're not just developing a career," Rosa would tell her. "You're creating entirely new languages of professional possibility."

Each professional challenge became an opportunity for deeper understanding. She didn't view career development as a competition, but as a sophisticated process of collective human potential expansion.

"Professional growth," she would tell her research team, "is about developing the capacity to see possibility where others see only limitation."

The Rodriguez family's immigrant background provided a crucial contextual framework. Generations had survived by developing an extraordinary capacity to read, interpret, and strategically navigate complex professional systems—transforming potential constraints into sites of innovation.

15.2 Breaking Professional Barriers

Professional barriers were never fixed obstacles for Elena Rodriguez. They were complex, adaptive systems waiting to be understood, reimagined, and transformed.

Her technological background provided a unique lens for understanding professional limitations. She approached institutional constraints with the same systematic curiosity she applied to complex technological systems. Each professional challenge became a dataset, each institutional barrier a system waiting to be redesigned.

Marcus, her research collaborator, was fascinated by her approach. "You're developing a technological understanding of career advancement," he observed. "Not just describing professional progress, but creating frameworks for intentional institutional transformation."

Elena developed what she called a "professional liberation framework"—a comprehensive approach to understanding and transcending institutional constraints. The framework had multiple sophisticated components:

1. **Institutional Topology**: Mapping complex professional ecosystems
2. **Adaptive Barrier Deconstruction**: Identifying and reimagining systemic limitations
3. **Transformative Professional Strategies**: Developing approaches to

institutional innovation

Her conversations with Gabriel became profound explorations of professional potential. They didn't just discuss career advancement. They created comprehensive models of how human beings could transform institutional constraints into sites of collective growth.

"Professional barriers," Gabriel would argue, "are often just poorly understood systems of potential human capability."

The technological tools Elena developed were extraordinary. Adaptive professional assessment platforms that could recognize complex patterns of institutional limitation and potential, that could create personalized strategies for breaking through systemic constraints.

But these were never just about technological solutions. They were always about human potential, about creating broader pathways of professional liberation and collective innovation.

Her work began to attract international attention. Organizational researchers, technological innovators, and social transformation experts all recognized that she was developing something far more profound than traditional career advancement methodologies. She was creating a comprehensive approach to understanding human professional potential.

15.3 The Pursuit of Professional Excellence

Ambition for Elena Rodriguez was never about individual achievement. It was a sophisticated ecosystem of collective potential—a continuous process of reimagining professional possibility that extended far beyond personal success.

Her approach to professional excellence challenged every traditional understanding of career development. Where conventional narratives saw ambition as a competitive pursuit, Elena saw it as a collaborative journey of collective human potential expansion.

The technological platforms she developed merged sophisticated machine learning algorithms with deep organizational psychology insights. These weren't just career assessment tools. They were comprehensive ecosystems of professional potential—platforms that could recognize complex institutional patterns and create transformative strategies.

"Professional excellence," she would explain to her research team, "is about developing the capacity to create institutional possibilities where others see only limitations."

Her mother Maria's wisdom echoed in these moments of profound professional exploration. "True ambition," Maria would say, "is not about personal achievement. It's about creating space for collective growth."

Rosa Martinez observed this transformation with profound appreciation. "You're not just pursuing professional excellence," Rosa would tell her. "You're creating entire new ecosystems of institutional possibility."

Elena's work demonstrated that ambition was a sophisticated form of collective imagination. Each professional challenge became an opportunity for deeper understanding, for more nuanced institutional and organizational integration.

The boundaries between personal growth, technological innovation, and professional understanding became increasingly fluid. Elena Rodriguez was not just a researcher or a technologist. She was an architect of professional possibility, continuously reimagining the very concept of human institutional potential.

Her platforms were never just about technological solutions. They were always about human potential, about creating broader pathways of professional liberation and creative reimagination.

As professional landscapes continued to shift and transform, Elena Rodriguez stood at their complex intersection—not as an observer, but as a creative force of continuous professional exploration.

Her approach was fundamentally revolutionary. Professional ambition was not about achieving a fixed state of individual success. It was about creating comprehensive ecosystems of collective potential, about developing broader pathways of continuous human and institutional growth.

Ambition, she was demonstrating, was never a destination. It was always a journey of endless, beautiful becoming—a continuous process of creating more expansive, more compassionate ways of understanding human professional potential.

In the intricate dance of professional development, Elena Rodriguez had discovered something profound: that true excellence was not about individual achievement. It was about creating institutional landscapes that allowed every individual to discover and expand their most authentic, most transformative potential.

Chapter 16: Moral Dilemmas

16.1 Ethical Crossroads

The landscape of moral complexity was never a simple terrain for Elena Rodriguez. It was an intricate, multidimensional ecosystem of ethical considerations—a sophisticated intersection of personal integrity, systemic constraints, and profound human potential.

Her approach to moral challenges emerged from the same analytical framework she applied to her technological and psychological research. Ethics were not a fixed set of rules, but a dynamic, continuously evolving process of understanding and reimagining human potential.

Carlos Rodriguez, her father, had been her first teacher of ethical navigation. "Moral choices," he would say, his engineering schematics spread across the kitchen table, "are never about simple right or wrong. They're about understanding complex systems of human potential."

The Rodriguez family's immigrant experience had been a crucible of ethical complexity. Survival had demanded more than rigid moral principles—it required a nuanced understanding of ethical adaptation, an ability to maintain personal integrity while navigating challenging systemic constraints.

Gabriel, her intellectual companion, recognized the extraordinary depth of her ethical exploration. "You don't just analyze moral challenges," he would observe during their deep conversations. "You systematically deconstruct the complex ecosystems of ethical decision-making."

Elena's technological platforms began to develop sophisticated moral assessment tools. These were not simple ethical frameworks or binary decision matrices. They were comprehensive ecosystems of moral intelligence—platforms that could recognize the intricate dynamics of ethical complexity.

"Moral navigation," she would explain to her research team, "is about developing a comprehensive understanding of ethical ecosystems. It's about recognizing the profound potential for ethical growth that exists within complex human experiences."

Rosa Martinez, her longtime mentor, saw something extraordinary in Elena's approach to ethical challenges. "You're creating entirely new languages of moral possibility," Rosa would tell her, her eyes reflecting a deep understanding of ethical complexity.

Each moral challenge became a site of profound research. Not in a detached, academic sense, but as a genuine exploration of human ethical potential. Elena understood that moral growth was never about rigid adherence to fixed principles. It was about creating expansive spaces of ethical understanding and collective growth.

Her work challenged traditional notions of ethical decision-making. Morality was not a fixed state to be achieved, but a continuous process of ethical and intellectual co-creation.

16.2 Navigating Ethical Complexities

Ethical complexities for Elena were never simple binary experiences. They were sophisticated, multilayered ecosystems of moral reasoning—complex networks of potential ethical transformation.

Her technological background provided a unique lens for understanding moral challenges. She approached ethical dilemmas with the same systematic curiosity she applied to complex technological systems. Each moral challenge became a dataset, each moment of ethical reflection a system waiting to be understood and reimagined.

Marcus, her research collaborator, was fascinated by her approach. "You're developing a technological understanding of moral decision-making," he observed. "Not just describing ethical challenges, but creating frameworks for intentional ethical evolution."

Elena developed what she called an "ethical complexity framework"—a comprehensive approach to understanding the profound intricacies of moral decision-making. The framework had multiple sophisticated components:

1. **Moral Topology**: Mapping the intricate landscapes of ethical reasoning
2. **Adaptive Ethical Modeling**: Creating flexible frameworks for moral growth
3. **Transformative Integrity Strategies**: Developing approaches to

continuous ethical evolution

Her conversations with Gabriel became profound explorations of moral complexity. They didn't just discuss ethical challenges. They created comprehensive models of how human beings could transform moral dilemmas into sites of collective ethical growth.

"Ethical complexity," Gabriel would argue, "is about recognizing the extraordinary potential for moral transformation that exists within genuine human experience."

The technological tools Elena developed were extraordinary. Adaptive ethical assessment platforms that could recognize complex patterns of moral limitation and potential, that could create personalized strategies for deepening ethical understanding.

But these were never just about technological solutions. They were always about human potential, about creating broader pathways of ethical liberation and moral depth.

Her work began to attract international attention. Philosophers, ethicists, and social transformation specialists all recognized that she was developing something far more profound than traditional moral frameworks. She was creating a comprehensive approach to understanding human ethical potential.

The Rodriguez family's immigrant background provided a crucial contextual framework. Generations had navigated complex moral landscapes, understanding that true ethical integrity was about survival, collective understanding, and continuous moral adaptation.

16.3 The Price of Moral Compromise

The consequences of moral compromise were never abstract theoretical concepts for Elena Rodriguez. They were lived experiences—profound explorations of the delicate balance between systemic survival and personal integrity.

Her approach to ethical consequences challenged every traditional moral narrative. Where conventional ethical frameworks presented morality as a fixed set of universal principles, Elena saw it as a dynamic ecosystem of continuous moral growth, a sophisticated space of collective ethical exploration.

The technological platforms she developed merged sophisticated machine learning algorithms with deep philosophical and psychological insights. These weren't just ethical assessment tools. They were comprehensive ecosystems of moral potential—platforms that could recognize complex ethical patterns and create transformative strategies for moral growth.

"Moral consequences," she would explain to her research team, "are about developing the capacity to see profound ethical potential where others see only surface-level ethical compromises."

Her mother Maria's wisdom echoed in these moments of profound ethical exploration. "True integrity," Maria would say, "is not about maintaining a perfect moral record. It's about creating space for continuous moral becoming."

Rosa Martinez observed this transformation with profound appreciation. "You're not just understanding ethical consequences," Rosa would tell her. "You're creating entire new ecosystems of moral possibility."

Elena's work demonstrated that moral growth was a sophisticated form of collective learning. Each ethical challenge became an opportunity for deeper understanding, for more nuanced moral and philosophical integration.

The boundaries between personal growth, technological innovation, and ethical understanding became increasingly fluid. Elena Rodriguez was not just a researcher or a technologist. She was an architect of moral possibility, continuously reimagining the very concept of human ethical potential.

Her platforms were never just about technological solutions. They were always about human potential, about creating broader pathways of ethical liberation and creative reimagination.

As moral landscapes continued to shift and transform, Elena Rodriguez stood at their complex intersection—not as an observer, but as a creative force of continuous ethical exploration.

Her approach was fundamentally revolutionary. Moral complexity was not about achieving a fixed state of ethical perfection. It was about creating comprehensive ecosystems of ethical possibility, about developing broader pathways of continuous human and collective moral growth.

Ethical consequences, she was demonstrating, were never a destination. They were always a journey of endless, beautiful becoming—a continuous process of creating more expansive, more compassionate ways of understanding human moral potential.

In the intricate dance of ethical decision-making, Elena Rodriguez had discovered something profound: that true moral integrity was not about maintaining a perfect ethical record. It was about creating spaces of collective understanding, about developing the capacity to grow, to learn, and to continuously reimagine the possibilities of human ethical potential.

Chapter 17: Intellectual Growth

17.1 Expanding Mental Horizons

The landscape of intellectual exploration was never a linear journey for Elena Rodriguez. It was a complex, multidimensional ecosystem of continuous learning—a sophisticated intersection of curiosity, technological innovation, and profound human potential.

Her approach to intellectual development emerged from the same analytical framework that defined every aspect of her life—a deep, systemic understanding that knowledge was not a destination, but a continuous process of creative reimagination.

Carlos Rodriguez, her father, had been her first mentor of intellectual strategy. "Learning," he would say, spreading out intricate engineering schematics across their modest kitchen table, "is not about accumulating information. It's about developing the capacity to see possibilities where others see limitations."

The Rodriguez family's immigrant experience had been a crucible of intellectual resilience. Survival had demanded more than traditional educational achievements—it required a nuanced ability to adapt, to think creatively, to transform intellectual constraints into opportunities for growth.

Gabriel, her intellectual companion, recognized the extraordinary depth of her mental exploration. "You don't just acquire knowledge," he would observe during their profound conversations. "You systematically deconstruct and reimagine entire intellectual ecosystems."

Elena's technological platforms began to develop sophisticated intellectual development tools. These were not simple learning management systems or traditional educational technologies. They were comprehensive ecosystems of intellectual potential—adaptive platforms that could recognize complex cognitive landscapes and create personalized learning strategies.

"Intellectual growth," she would explain to her research team, "is about developing the capacity to continuously expand our understanding of human potential."

Rosa Martinez, her longtime mentor, saw something extraordinary in Elena's approach to intellectual development. "You're creating entirely new languages of mental possibility," Rosa would tell her, her eyes reflecting a deep understanding of cognitive complexity.

Each intellectual challenge became a site of profound research. Not in a detached, academic sense, but as a genuine exploration of human cognitive potential. Elena understood that intellectual growth was never about accumulating facts or achieving fixed academic milestones. It was about creating expansive spaces of understanding and continuous learning.

Her work challenged traditional notions of intellectual development. Knowledge was not a static body of information to be mastered, but a continuous process of creative exploration and reimagination.

17.2 Challenging Intellectual Boundaries

Intellectual boundaries were never fixed limitations for Elena Rodriguez. They were complex, adaptive systems waiting to be understood, challenged, and transformed.

Her technological background provided a unique lens for understanding cognitive constraints. She approached intellectual limitations with the same systematic curiosity she applied to complex technological systems. Each intellectual challenge became a dataset, each cognitive boundary a system waiting to be redesigned and expanded.

Marcus, her research collaborator, was fascinated by her approach. "You're developing a technological understanding of intellectual growth," he observed. "Not just describing learning processes, but creating frameworks for intentional cognitive evolution."

Elena developed what she called an "intellectual liberation framework"—a comprehensive approach to understanding and transcending cognitive limitations. The framework had multiple sophisticated components:

1. **Cognitive Topology**: Mapping complex intellectual landscapes
2. **Adaptive Learning Deconstruction**: Identifying and reimagining cognitive constraints
3. **Transformative Intellectual Strategies**: Developing approaches to continuous mental expansion

Her conversations with Gabriel became profound explorations of intellectual potential. They didn't just discuss academic knowledge. They created comprehensive models of how human beings could transform intellectual boundaries into sites of collective cognitive growth.

"Intellectual boundaries," Gabriel would argue, "are often just poorly understood systems of human cognitive capability."

The technological tools Elena developed were extraordinary. Adaptive intellectual assessment platforms that could recognize complex patterns of cognitive limitation and potential, that could create personalized strategies for breaking through intellectual constraints.

But these were never just about technological solutions. They were always about human potential, about creating broader pathways of intellectual liberation and collective cognitive innovation.

Her work began to attract international attention. Educational researchers, cognitive scientists, and technological innovators all recognized that she was developing something far more profound than traditional learning methodologies. She was creating a comprehensive approach to understanding human intellectual potential.

The Rodriguez family's immigrant background provided a crucial contextual framework. Generations had navigated complex intellectual landscapes, understanding that true learning was about survival, collective understanding, and continuous cognitive adaptation.

17.3 The Pursuit of Knowledge

The pursuit of knowledge for Elena Rodriguez was never about academic achievement or intellectual accumulation. It was a sophisticated ecosystem of collective cognitive potential—a continuous process of reimagining intellectual possibility that extended far beyond individual learning.

Her approach to continuous learning challenged every traditional understanding of educational development. Where conventional narratives saw knowledge as a fixed body of information to be mastered, Elena saw it as a collaborative journey of collective human cognitive expansion.

The technological platforms she developed merged sophisticated machine learning algorithms with deep cognitive science and educational psychology insights. These weren't just learning assessment tools. They were comprehensive ecosystems of intellectual potential—platforms that could recognize complex cognitive patterns and create transformative strategies for continuous learning.

"Knowledge pursuit," she would explain to her research team, "is about developing the capacity to create intellectual possibilities where others see only limitations."

Her mother Maria's wisdom echoed in these moments of profound intellectual exploration. "True learning," Maria would say, "is not about accumulating information. It's about creating space for continuous cognitive growth."

Rosa Martinez observed this transformation with profound appreciation. "You're not just pursuing knowledge," Rosa would tell her. "You're creating entire new ecosystems of intellectual possibility."

Elena's work demonstrated that learning was a sophisticated form of collective imagination. Each intellectual challenge became an opportunity for deeper understanding, for more nuanced cognitive and creative integration.

The boundaries between personal growth, technological innovation, and intellectual understanding became increasingly fluid. Elena Rodriguez was not just a researcher or a technologist. She was an architect of intellectual possibility, continuously reimagining the very concept of human cognitive potential.

Her platforms were never just about technological solutions. They were always about human potential, about creating broader pathways of intellectual liberation and creative reimagination.

As intellectual landscapes continued to shift and transform, Elena Rodriguez stood at their complex intersection—not as an observer, but as a creative force of continuous intellectual exploration.

Her approach was fundamentally revolutionary. The pursuit of knowledge was not about achieving a fixed state of intellectual mastery. It was about creating comprehensive ecosystems of collective potential, about developing broader pathways of continuous human and cognitive growth.

Continuous learning, she was demonstrating, was never a destination. It was always a journey of endless, beautiful becoming—a continuous process of creating more expansive, more compassionate ways of understanding human intellectual potential.

In the intricate dance of knowledge pursuit, Elena Rodriguez had discovered something profound: that true intellectual growth was not about individual academic achievement. It was about creating cognitive landscapes that allowed every individual to discover and expand their most authentic, most transformative intellectual potential.

Chapter 18: Social Reinvention

18.1 Redefining Personal Identity

The process of self-transformation was never a simple reconstruction for Elena Rodriguez. It was a complex, multidimensional ecosystem of continuous reimagination—a sophisticated journey of personal reinvention that challenged every traditional understanding of identity.

Her approach to personal identity emerged from the intricate survival strategies of her immigrant family—a profound understanding that self-definition was not a fixed state, but a dynamic, continuously evolving process of creative potential.

Carlos Rodriguez had been her first mentor of personal transformation. "Identity," he would say, spreading out complex engineering schematics, "is not a blueprint to be followed. It's a living system to be continuously redesigned."

The Rodriguez family's immigrant experience had been a crucible of personal reinvention. Survival had demanded more than static self-understanding. It required a nuanced ability to adapt, to reimagine personal potential in the face of complex social and cultural constraints.

Gabriel, her intellectual companion, recognized the extraordinary depth of her identity exploration. "You don't just redefine yourself," he would observe during their profound conversations. "You systematically deconstruct and reimagine entire ecosystems of personal potential."

Elena's technological platforms began to develop sophisticated identity assessment tools. These were not simple personality tests or demographic categorizations. They were comprehensive ecosystems of personal potential—adaptive platforms that could recognize complex identity landscapes and create personalized transformation strategies.

"Social reinvention," she would explain to her research team, "is about developing the capacity to continuously expand our understanding of human potential beyond fixed social categories."

Rosa Martinez, her longtime mentor, saw something extraordinary in Elena's approach to personal transformation. "You're creating entirely new languages of identity possibility," Rosa would tell her, her eyes reflecting a deep understanding of social complexity.

Each moment of personal reinvention became a site of profound research. Not in a detached, academic sense, but as a genuine exploration of human potential for continuous becoming. Elena understood that identity was never about achieving a fixed state of self-definition. It was about creating expansive spaces of personal possibility.

Her work challenged traditional notions of social identity. Personal definition was not a static construct to be discovered, but a continuous process of creative reimagination and social navigation.

18.2 Breaking Social Expectations

Social expectations were never immutable boundaries for Elena Rodriguez. They were complex, adaptive systems waiting to be understood, challenged, and transformed.

Her technological background provided a unique lens for understanding social constraints. She approached societal expectations with the same systematic curiosity she applied to complex technological systems. Each social limitation became a dataset, each institutional expectation a system waiting to be redesigned and expanded.

Marcus, her research collaborator, was fascinated by her approach. "You're developing a technological understanding of social transformation," he observed. "Not just describing personal rebellion, but creating frameworks for intentional social evolution."

Elena developed what she called a "social liberation framework"—a comprehensive approach to understanding and transcending social expectations. The framework had multiple sophisticated components:

1. **Social Topology**: Mapping complex social landscapes of expectation
2. **Adaptive Identity Deconstruction**: Identifying and reimagining social constraints
3. **Transformative Personal Strategies**: Developing approaches to continuous social reinvention

Her conversations with Gabriel became profound explorations of personal potential beyond social limitations. They didn't just discuss social expectations. They created comprehensive models of how human beings could transform social constraints into sites of collective personal growth.

"Social expectations," Gabriel would argue, "are often just poorly understood systems of human potential limitation."

The technological tools Elena developed were extraordinary. Adaptive social assessment platforms that could recognize complex patterns of social limitation and potential, that could create personalized strategies for breaking through societal constraints.

But these were never just about technological solutions. They were always about human potential, about creating broader pathways of personal liberation and collective social innovation.

Her work began to attract international attention. Sociologists, anthropologists, and social transformation experts all recognized that she was developing something far more profound than traditional identity frameworks. She was creating a comprehensive approach to understanding human social potential.

The Rodriguez family's immigrant background provided a crucial contextual framework. Generations had navigated complex social landscapes, understanding that true personal liberation was about survival, collective understanding, and continuous social adaptation.

18.3 Crafting a New Social Persona

The crafting of a new social persona was never about surface-level transformation for Elena Rodriguez. It was a sophisticated ecosystem of personal potential—a continuous process of reimagining social identity that extended far beyond traditional notions of self-reinvention.

Her approach to identity reconstruction challenged every traditional understanding of social definition. Where conventional narratives saw personal identity as a fixed construct, Elena saw it as a dynamic, collaborative journey of collective human potential expansion.

The technological platforms she developed merged sophisticated machine learning algorithms with deep sociological and psychological insights. These weren't just identity assessment tools. They were comprehensive ecosystems of personal potential—platforms that could recognize complex social patterns and create transformative strategies for continuous personal reinvention.

"Social persona crafting," she would explain to her research team, "is about developing the capacity to create personal possibilities where others see only social limitations."

Her mother Maria's wisdom echoed in these moments of profound personal exploration. "True transformation," Maria would say, "is not about rejecting your origins. It's about creating space for continuous personal becoming."

Rosa Martinez observed this transformation with profound appreciation. "You're not just reconstructing your identity," Rosa would tell her. "You're creating entire new ecosystems of personal possibility."

Elena's work demonstrated that personal reinvention was a sophisticated form of collective imagination. Each social challenge became an opportunity for deeper understanding, for more nuanced personal and social integration.

The boundaries between personal growth, technological innovation, and social understanding became increasingly fluid. Elena Rodriguez was not just a researcher or a technologist. She was an architect of personal possibility, continuously reimagining the very concept of human social potential.

Her platforms were never just about technological solutions. They were always about human potential, about creating broader pathways of personal liberation and creative reimagination.

As social landscapes continued to shift and transform, Elena Rodriguez stood at their complex intersection—not as an observer, but as a creative force of continuous personal exploration.

Her approach was fundamentally revolutionary. Social reinvention was not about achieving a fixed state of personal definition. It was about creating comprehensive ecosystems of personal potential, about developing broader pathways of continuous human and social growth.

Identity reconstruction, she was demonstrating, was never a destination. It was always a journey of endless, beautiful becoming—a continuous process of creating more expansive, more compassionate ways of understanding human social potential.

In the intricate dance of personal reinvention, Elena Rodriguez had discovered something profound: that true social transformation was not about rejecting one's origins or achieving a perfect social persona. It was about creating spaces of personal understanding, about developing the capacity to grow, to learn, and to continuously reimagine the possibilities of human social potential.

Chapter 19: Emotional Intelligence

19.1 Understanding Emotional Dynamics

The landscape of emotional understanding was never a simple terrain for Elena Rodriguez. It was a complex, multidimensional ecosystem of psychological exploration—a sophisticated intersection of self-awareness, technological innovation, and profound human potential.

Her approach to emotional dynamics emerged from the intricate survival strategies of her immigrant family—a deep understanding that emotional intelligence was not a fixed trait, but a dynamic, continuously evolving process of psychological navigation.

Carlos Rodriguez had been her first mentor of emotional strategy. "Emotions," he would say, drawing intricate diagrams alongside his engineering schematics, "are not weaknesses to be controlled. They are sophisticated information systems waiting to be understood."

The Rodriguez family's immigrant experience had been a crucible of emotional resilience. Survival had demanded more than emotional suppression—it required a nuanced ability to read, interpret, and transform emotional landscapes with extraordinary precision.

Gabriel, her intellectual companion, recognized the extraordinary depth of her emotional exploration. "You don't just analyze emotions," he would observe during their profound conversations. "You systematically deconstruct and reimagine entire emotional ecosystems."

Elena's technological platforms began to develop sophisticated emotional intelligence tools. These were not simple mood tracking applications or basic psychological assessments. They were comprehensive ecosystems of emotional potential—adaptive platforms that could recognize complex emotional landscapes and create personalized emotional understanding strategies.

"Emotional dynamics," she would explain to her research team, "are about developing the capacity to continuously expand our understanding of human psychological potential."

Rosa Martinez, her longtime mentor, saw something extraordinary in Elena's approach to emotional understanding. "You're creating entirely new languages of psychological possibility," Rosa would tell her, her eyes reflecting a deep understanding of emotional complexity.

Each emotional challenge became a site of profound research. Not in a clinical, detached sense, but as a genuine exploration of human psychological potential. Elena understood that emotional intelligence was never about achieving a fixed state of psychological control. It was about creating expansive spaces of emotional understanding and continuous growth.

Her work challenged traditional notions of emotional management. Emotions were not simply reactions to be regulated, but sophisticated information systems that offered profound insights into human potential.

19.2 Mastering Emotional Responses

Emotional responses were never simple reactive mechanisms for Elena Rodriguez. They were complex, adaptive systems waiting to be understood, interpreted, and transformed.

Her technological background provided a unique lens for understanding emotional complexity. She approached emotional regulation with the same systematic curiosity she applied to complex technological systems. Each emotional response became a dataset, each psychological pattern a system waiting to be redesigned and expanded.

Marcus, her research collaborator, was fascinated by her approach. "You're developing a technological understanding of emotional intelligence," he observed. "Not just describing emotional responses, but creating frameworks for intentional psychological evolution."

Elena developed what she called an "emotional liberation framework"—a comprehensive approach to understanding and transforming emotional responses. The framework had multiple sophisticated components:

1. **Emotional Topology**: Mapping complex psychological landscapes
2. **Adaptive Response Deconstruction**: Identifying and reimagining emotional patterns
3. **Transformative Emotional Strategies**: Developing approaches to continuous psychological growth

Her conversations with Gabriel became profound explorations of emotional potential. They didn't just discuss emotional regulation. They created comprehensive models of how human beings could transform emotional challenges into sites of collective psychological growth.

"Emotional responses," Gabriel would argue, "are often just poorly understood systems of human psychological capability."

The technological tools Elena developed were extraordinary. Adaptive emotional assessment platforms that could recognize complex patterns of psychological limitation and potential, that could create personalized strategies for transforming emotional responses.

But these were never just about technological solutions. They were always about human potential, about creating broader pathways of emotional liberation and collective psychological innovation.

Her work began to attract international attention. Psychologists, neuroscientists, and social transformation experts all recognized that she was developing something far more profound than traditional emotional regulation methodologies. She was creating a comprehensive approach to understanding human emotional potential.

The Rodriguez family's immigrant background provided a crucial contextual framework. Generations had navigated complex emotional landscapes, understanding that true emotional mastery was about survival, collective understanding, and continuous psychological adaptation.

19.3 The Power of Emotional Insight

The pursuit of emotional insight was never about achieving emotional perfection for Elena Rodriguez. It was a sophisticated ecosystem of psychological potential—a continuous process of reimagining emotional understanding that extended far beyond traditional notions of emotional intelligence.

Her approach to psychological understanding challenged every traditional emotional management narrative. Where conventional approaches saw emotions as problems to be solved, Elena saw them as complex information systems offering profound insights into human potential.

The technological platforms she developed merged sophisticated machine learning algorithms with deep psychological and neuroscientific insights. These weren't just emotional assessment tools. They were comprehensive ecosystems of psychological potential—platforms that could recognize complex emotional patterns and create transformative strategies for continuous emotional growth.

"Emotional insight," she would explain to her research team, "is about developing the capacity to create psychological possibilities where others see only emotional limitations."

Her mother Maria's wisdom echoed in these moments of profound emotional exploration. "True understanding," Maria would say, "is not about controlling emotions. It's about creating space for continuous psychological becoming."

Rosa Martinez observed this transformation with profound appreciation. "You're not just analyzing emotions," Rosa would tell her. "You're creating entire new ecosystems of psychological possibility."

Elena's work demonstrated that emotional insight was a sophisticated form of collective imagination. Each emotional challenge became an opportunity for deeper understanding, for more nuanced psychological and emotional integration.

The boundaries between personal growth, technological innovation, and psychological understanding became increasingly fluid. Elena Rodriguez was not just a researcher or a technologist. She was an architect of emotional possibility, continuously reimagining the very concept of human psychological potential.

Her platforms were never just about technological solutions. They were always about human potential, about creating broader pathways of emotional liberation and creative reimagination.

As emotional landscapes continued to shift and transform, Elena Rodriguez stood at their complex intersection—not as an observer, but as a creative force of continuous psychological exploration.

Her approach was fundamentally revolutionary. Emotional understanding was not about achieving a fixed state of psychological control. It was about creating comprehensive ecosystems of emotional potential, about developing broader pathways of continuous human and psychological growth.

Emotional insight, she was demonstrating, was never a destination. It was always a journey of endless, beautiful becoming—a continuous process of creating more expansive, more compassionate ways of understanding human psychological potential.

In the intricate dance of emotional exploration, Elena Rodriguez had discovered something profound: that true emotional intelligence was not about perfect emotional control. It was about creating spaces of psychological understanding, about developing the capacity to grow, to learn, and to continuously reimagine the possibilities of human emotional potential.

Chapter 20: Love and Ambition

20.1 Balancing Personal Desires

The intersection of love and ambition was never a simple terrain for Elena Rodriguez. It was a complex psychological landscape where personal desires, romantic aspirations, and professional dreams converged in a delicate, sometimes volatile dance of emotional and strategic negotiation.

Gabriel Santos had always been more than just a romantic partner. He was an intellectual companion, a strategic ally in Elena's journey of continuous psychological and professional exploration. Their relationship was not a traditional romantic narrative of compromise and submission, but a sophisticated ecosystem of mutual growth, challenge, and profound emotional understanding.

"Love," Gabriel would often say during their profound late-night conversations, "is not about finding someone who completes you. It's about finding someone who expansively challenges your understanding of personal potential."

Their first significant encounter had been at an international conference on technological innovation and social transformation. Elena was presenting her groundbreaking work on adaptive emotional intelligence platforms, and Gabriel was leading a panel on technological ethics and human potential. Their intellectual connection was instantaneous—a recognition of kindred spirits who saw the world not as it was, but as it could be.

Rosa Martinez, Elena's longtime mentor, observed their relationship with a nuanced understanding. "Your connection," she told them, "is not about romantic possession. It's about creating collective spaces of psychological and professional possibility."

The Rodriguez family's immigrant background had always emphasized love as a strategic and emotional collaboration. Love was never a passive experience but an active process of mutual growth, of creating broader pathways of collective potential. Carlos and Maria Rodriguez had demonstrated this throughout their lives—their partnership was a profound negotiation of individual dreams and shared survival strategies.

Elena and Gabriel's relationship became a laboratory of emotional and professional exploration. They didn't just support each other's ambitions; they actively co-created frameworks for continuous personal and collective transformation.

Their romantic connection challenged every traditional narrative of love. It wasn't about finding security or creating a conventional domestic space. It was about expanding the very boundaries of what romantic partnership could represent—a dynamic, evolving ecosystem of mutual intellectual and emotional growth.

"We are not just partners," Gabriel would tell her. "We are collaborative architects of psychological possibility."

20.2 Navigating Romantic Challenges

The challenges of their relationship were never simple personal conflicts. They were sophisticated negotiations of individual potential, professional ambition, and emotional complexity.

Their first major professional collaboration came when Elena's emotional intelligence platforms intersected with Gabriel's work on technological ethics. They weren't just romantic partners working together; they were creating entirely new frameworks of understanding human potential.

The project was groundbreaking—a comprehensive approach to developing technological tools that could recognize and support individual emotional growth while maintaining strict ethical boundaries. It wasn't just about creating another technological solution. It was about reimagining the very relationship between human emotional potential and technological innovation.

Marcus, their research collaborator, was fascinated by their collaborative approach. "You're not just developing a technological platform," he observed. "You're creating an entire philosophical ecosystem of emotional and technological possibility."

Their romantic challenges were never about traditional relationship tensions. They were about navigating the complex terrains of individual ambition, collective potential, and the continuous negotiation of personal and professional boundaries.

When Elena received an international research grant that would require her to spend six months in a cutting-edge research facility in Singapore, their relationship underwent a profound transformation. Instead of viewing this as a potential threat to their connection, they saw it as an opportunity for individual and collective growth.

"Distance," Gabriel wrote in a deeply reflective email, "is not about separation. It's about creating expanded spaces of personal and collective potential."

Their communication during this period was extraordinary. Daily video conversations became profound explorations of their individual research, their emotional landscapes, and their collective vision. They weren't just maintaining a long-distance relationship; they were continuously co-creating new frameworks of romantic and professional understanding.

Elena's research in Singapore explored the intersection of machine learning, emotional intelligence, and cross-cultural psychological adaptation. Gabriel's parallel work in ethical technology development complemented her research in extraordinary ways. They weren't just supporting each other's work; they were creating collaborative ecosystems of technological and emotional innovation.

The Rodriguez family saw their relationship as a profound evolution of romantic possibility. It wasn't about traditional notions of love and partnership. It was about creating broader pathways of collective human potential.

20.3 Love as a Transformative Force

Love, for Elena Rodriguez, was never a static emotional state. It was a dynamic, continuously evolving process of mutual psychological and professional transformation.

Her work with Gabriel demonstrated that love could be a sophisticated technological and emotional framework—a collaborative process of continuous personal and collective growth. Their relationship became a living laboratory of emotional and professional exploration.

The technological platforms they developed together were extraordinary. Adaptive systems that could recognize not just individual emotional patterns, but the complex emotional dynamics of collaborative human potential. These were not just research tools. They were philosophical ecosystems that challenged traditional understanding of human connection.

"Love," Elena would explain to her research team, "is about creating expansive spaces of mutual psychological becoming."

Their connection transcended traditional romantic narratives. It wasn't about finding emotional comfort or creating a conventional domestic framework. It was about continuously reimagining the possibilities of human connection, about developing more sophisticated, more compassionate ways of understanding individual and collective potential.

Gabriel's perspective complemented Elena's extraordinary vision. "Romantic connection," he would argue, "is not about emotional possession. It's about creating collaborative ecosystems of psychological and professional possibility."

The technological tools they developed together were never just about solving emotional challenges. They were about creating broader pathways of human understanding, about developing more nuanced, more compassionate frameworks of emotional and professional exploration.

Their love story was a profound reimagining of romantic possibility. It demonstrated that love could be a revolutionary force—a collaborative process of continuous personal and collective transformation.

As technological and emotional landscapes continued to shift and transform, Elena Rodriguez and Gabriel Santos stood at their complex intersection—not as traditional romantic partners, but as collaborative architects of human potential.

Their approach was fundamentally revolutionary. Love was not a destination. It was always a journey of endless, beautiful becoming—a continuous process of creating more expansive, more compassionate ways of understanding human connection.

In the intricate dance of romantic and professional exploration, they had discovered something profound: that true love was not about emotional possession or traditional partnership. It was about creating spaces of mutual understanding, about developing the capacity to grow, to learn, and to continuously reimagine the possibilities of human potential.

Their connection was a testament to the transformative power of love—not as a passive emotional state, but as an active, dynamic force of continuous personal and collective evolution.

Chapter 21: Professional Challenges

21.1 Overcoming Career Obstacles

The landscape of professional advancement was never a linear trajectory for Elena Rodriguez. It was a complex, multidimensional terrain of strategic navigation, continuous learning, and profound psychological transformation.

Her professional journey emerged from the intricate survival strategies of her immigrant family—a deep understanding that career success was not about individual achievement, but about creating comprehensive ecosystems of collective potential. The Rodriguez family had always understood that professional challenges were sophisticated opportunities for growth, not mere obstacles to be overcome.

Carlos Rodriguez, her father, had been her first mentor of professional strategy. "A career," he would say, drawing intricate diagrams that blended engineering precision with philosophical insight, "is not a ladder to climb, but an ecosystem to cultivate."

The technological platforms Elena developed were far more than professional tools. They were comprehensive frameworks of professional possibility—adaptive systems that could recognize complex career challenges and create personalized strategies for continuous professional evolution.

Her relationship with Gabriel Santos provided a unique collaborative lens for understanding professional complexity. They didn't just support each other's careers; they created collaborative ecosystems of professional potential.

Rosa Martinez, her longtime mentor, recognized the extraordinary depth of Elena's professional exploration. "You're not just navigating a career," Rosa would observe during their profound conversations. "You're systematically deconstructing and reimagining entire professional landscapes."

Each professional challenge became a site of profound research. Not in a clinical, detached sense, but as a genuine exploration of human professional potential. Elena understood that professional growth was never about achieving a fixed state of success. It was about creating expansive spaces of continuous learning and transformation.

Her work challenged traditional notions of career development. Professional challenges were not simply problems to be solved, but sophisticated information systems that offered profound insights into human potential.

The international research grant that took her to Singapore was more than a professional opportunity. It was a comprehensive exploration of technological and psychological boundaries. Elena's research explored the intricate intersections of machine learning, emotional intelligence, and cross-cultural professional adaptation.

Her approach was fundamentally revolutionary. Professional challenges were not obstacles, but sophisticated opportunities for psychological and technological innovation.

21.2 Strategic Career Navigation

Professional strategy was never a simple linear progression for Elena Rodriguez. It was a complex, adaptive system of continuous learning, strategic positioning, and profound psychological transformation.

The technological background she had inherited from her engineering family provided a unique lens for understanding professional complexity. She approached career navigation with the same systematic curiosity she applied to complex technological systems. Each professional challenge became a dataset, each career transition a system waiting to be redesigned and expanded.

Marcus, her research collaborator, was fascinated by her approach. "You're developing a comprehensive framework of professional evolution," he observed. "Not just advancing a career, but creating entire ecosystems of professional potential."

Elena developed what she called a "professional liberation framework"—a comprehensive approach to understanding and transforming career trajectories. The framework had multiple sophisticated components:

1. **Professional Topology**: Mapping complex career landscapes
2. **Strategic Adaptation Mechanisms**: Identifying and reimagining professional patterns
3. **Transformative Career Strategies**: Developing approaches to continuous professional growth

Her conversations with Gabriel became profound explorations of professional potential. They didn't just discuss career advancement. They created comprehensive models of how human beings could transform professional challenges into sites of collective innovation.

"Professional development," Gabriel would argue, "is often just poorly understood systems of human capability."

The technological tools Elena developed were extraordinary. Adaptive professional assessment platforms that could recognize complex patterns of professional limitation and potential, that could create personalized strategies for transforming career trajectories.

But these were never just about technological solutions. They were always about human potential, about creating broader pathways of professional liberation and collective innovation.

Her work began to attract international attention. Technology experts, organizational psychologists, and innovation strategists all recognized that she was developing something far more profound than traditional career development methodologies. She was creating a comprehensive approach to understanding human professional potential.

The Rodriguez family's immigrant background provided a crucial contextual framework. Generations had navigated complex professional landscapes, understanding that true professional mastery was about survival, collective understanding, and continuous adaptation.

International conferences became sites of extraordinary professional exploration. Elena wasn't just presenting research; she was creating comprehensive dialogues about the future of human potential, technological innovation, and professional evolution.

21.3 The Pursuit of Professional Fulfillment

The pursuit of professional fulfillment was never about achieving career perfection for Elena Rodriguez. It was a sophisticated ecosystem of professional potential—a continuous process of reimagining professional understanding that extended far beyond traditional notions of career development.

Her approach to professional growth challenged every conventional career management narrative. Where traditional approaches saw professional challenges as problems to be solved, Elena saw them as complex information systems offering profound insights into human potential.

The technological platforms she developed merged sophisticated machine learning algorithms with deep organizational psychology and innovation research. These weren't just career assessment tools. They were comprehensive ecosystems of professional potential—platforms that could recognize complex professional patterns and create transformative strategies for continuous career growth.

"Professional fulfillment," she would explain to her research team, "is about developing the capacity to create professional possibilities where others see only limitations."

Her mother Maria's wisdom echoed in these moments of profound professional exploration. "True professional growth," Maria would say, "is not about achieving a specific position. It's about creating space for continuous professional becoming."

Rosa Martinez observed this transformation with profound appreciation. "You're not just analyzing career trajectories," Rosa would tell her. "You're creating entire new ecosystems of professional possibility."

Elena's work demonstrated that professional fulfillment was a sophisticated form of collective imagination. Each professional challenge became an opportunity for deeper understanding, for more nuanced professional and technological integration.

The boundaries between personal growth, technological innovation, and professional development became increasingly fluid. Elena Rodriguez was not just a researcher or a technologist. She was an architect of professional possibility, continuously reimagining the very concept of human professional potential.

Her platforms were never just about technological solutions. They were always about human potential, about creating broader pathways of professional liberation and creative reimagination.

As professional landscapes continued to shift and transform, Elena Rodriguez stood at their complex intersection—not as an observer, but as a creative force of continuous professional exploration.

Her approach was fundamentally revolutionary. Professional fulfillment was not about achieving a fixed state of career success. It was about creating comprehensive ecosystems of professional potential, about developing broader pathways of continuous human and technological growth.

Professional development, she was demonstrating, was never a destination. It was always a journey of endless, beautiful becoming—a continuous process of creating more expansive, more innovative ways of understanding human professional potential.

In the intricate dance of professional exploration, Elena Rodriguez had discovered something profound: that true professional fulfillment was not about perfect career progression. It was about creating spaces of professional understanding, about developing the capacity to grow, to learn, and to continuously reimagine the possibilities of human professional potential.

Chapter 22: Psychological Barriers

22.1 Identifying Internal Limitations

The most profound borders were never external for Elena Rodriguez. They existed within the intricate landscapes of psychological possibility—invisible boundaries that constrained human potential, waiting to be recognized, challenged, and ultimately transformed.

Every psychological barrier was a complex ecosystem of inherited narratives, cultural constraints, and deeply embedded belief systems. Elena understood that these limitations were not fixed structures, but adaptive systems waiting to be decoded, reimagined, and ultimately liberated.

Her mother Maria had been the first to illuminate these internal landscapes. "The most challenging boundaries," she would say, her hands tracing invisible maps of psychological terrain, "are the ones we create for ourselves, often without even recognizing their existence."

The Rodriguez family's immigrant experience had been a profound teacher of psychological resilience. Survival had demanded more than external adaptation—it required a nuanced ability to recognize and dismantle internal psychological constraints.

Gabriel Santos recognized the extraordinary depth of her psychological exploration. "You don't just analyze psychological barriers," he would observe during their profound conversations. "You systematically deconstruct entire ecosystems of self-limitation."

Her technological platforms began to develop sophisticated psychological mapping tools. These were not simple self-assessment applications or basic psychological inventories. They were comprehensive ecosystems of psychological potential—adaptive platforms that could recognize complex internal limitation patterns and create personalized strategies for psychological liberation.

"Psychological barriers," she would explain to her research team, "are sophisticated information systems of inherited limitations waiting to be understood and transformed."

Rosa Martinez saw something extraordinary in Elena's approach to psychological exploration. "You're creating entirely new languages of psychological possibility," Rosa would tell her, her eyes reflecting a deep understanding of internal complexity.

Each psychological barrier became a site of profound research. Not in a clinical, detached sense, but as a genuine exploration of human psychological potential. Elena understood that internal limitations were never fixed states to be accepted. They were dynamic systems waiting to be reimagined.

Her work challenged traditional notions of psychological assessment. Psychological barriers were not simply problems to be solved, but sophisticated information systems that offered profound insights into human potential for transformation.

The technological tools she developed were extraordinary. They didn't just identify psychological limitations; they created comprehensive frameworks for understanding how these limitations were constructed, maintained, and ultimately could be deconstructed.

Carlos Rodriguez's engineering background had taught her that every system, no matter how complex, could be understood, mapped, and reimagined. Psychological barriers were no different—they were intricate systems waiting for a sophisticated approach of understanding and transformation.

22.2 Breaking Psychological Constraints

Psychological liberation was never a simple process of elimination for Elena Rodriguez. It was a complex, adaptive strategy of recognition, deconstruction, and creative reimagination.

Her technological background provided a unique lens for understanding psychological complexity. She approached psychological constraints with the same systematic curiosity she applied to complex technological systems. Each psychological pattern became a dataset, each internal limitation a system waiting to be redesigned and expanded.

Marcus, her research collaborator, was fascinated by her approach. "You're developing a technological understanding of psychological liberation," he observed. "Not just describing internal constraints, but creating frameworks for intentional psychological evolution."

Elena developed what she called a "psychological liberation framework"—a comprehensive approach to understanding and transforming internal limitations. The framework had multiple sophisticated components:

1. **Psychological Mapping**: Identifying complex internal constraint systems
2. **Narrative Deconstruction**: Analyzing inherited psychological patterns
3. **Transformative Reconstruction**: Developing strategies for internal reimagination

Her conversations with Gabriel became profound explorations of psychological potential. They didn't just discuss breaking psychological barriers. They created comprehensive models of how human beings could transform internal limitations into sites of collective psychological growth.

"Psychological constraints," Gabriel would argue, "are often just poorly understood systems of human capability."

The technological tools Elena developed were extraordinary. Adaptive psychological assessment platforms that could recognize complex patterns of internal limitation, that could create personalized strategies for transforming psychological constraints.

But these were never just about technological solutions. They were always about human potential, about creating broader pathways of psychological liberation and collective innovation.

Her work began to attract international attention. Psychologists, neuroscientists, and social transformation experts all recognized that she was developing something far more profound than traditional psychological assessment methodologies. She was creating a comprehensive approach to understanding human psychological potential.

The Rodriguez family's immigrant background provided a crucial contextual framework. Generations had navigated complex psychological landscapes, understanding that true psychological liberation was about survival, collective understanding, and continuous adaptation.

International research collaborations became sites of extraordinary psychological exploration. Elena wasn't just studying psychological constraints;

she was creating comprehensive dialogues about the future of human potential and psychological transformation.

22.3 The Journey of Self-Discovery

The journey of self-discovery was never a destination for Elena Rodriguez. It was a sophisticated ecosystem of psychological potential—a continuous process of reimagining psychological understanding that extended far beyond traditional notions of personal development.

Her approach to psychological exploration challenged every conventional narrative of self-understanding. Where traditional approaches saw self-discovery as a linear process, Elena saw it as a complex, adaptive system of continuous transformation.

The technological platforms she developed merged sophisticated machine learning algorithms with deep psychological and neuroscientific insights. These weren't just self-assessment tools. They were comprehensive ecosystems of psychological potential—platforms that could recognize complex internal patterns and create transformative strategies for continuous psychological growth.

"Self-discovery," she would explain to her research team, "is about developing the capacity to create psychological possibilities where others see only limitations."

Her mother Maria's wisdom echoed in these moments of profound psychological exploration. "True understanding," Maria would say, "is not about fixing oneself. It's about creating space for continuous psychological becoming."

Rosa Martinez observed this transformation with profound appreciation. "You're not just analyzing psychological patterns," Rosa would tell her. "You're creating entire new ecosystems of psychological possibility."

Elena's work demonstrated that self-discovery was a sophisticated form of collective imagination. Each psychological challenge became an opportunity for deeper understanding, for more nuanced psychological and emotional integration.

The boundaries between personal growth, technological innovation, and psychological understanding became increasingly fluid. Elena Rodriguez was not just a researcher or a technologist. She was an architect of psychological possibility, continuously reimagining the very concept of human psychological potential.

Her platforms were never just about technological solutions. They were always about human potential, about creating broader pathways of psychological liberation and creative reimagination.

As psychological landscapes continued to shift and transform, Elena Rodriguez stood at their complex intersection—not as an observer, but as a creative force of continuous psychological exploration.

Her approach was fundamentally revolutionary. Self-discovery was not about achieving a fixed state of psychological understanding. It was about creating comprehensive ecosystems of psychological potential, about developing broader pathways of continuous human and psychological growth.

Psychological exploration, she was demonstrating, was never a destination. It was always a journey of endless, beautiful becoming—a continuous process of creating more expansive, more compassionate ways of understanding human psychological potential.

In the intricate dance of psychological exploration, Elena Rodriguez had discovered something profound: that true self-discovery was not about perfect self-understanding. It was about creating spaces of psychological understanding, about developing the capacity to grow, to learn, and to continuously reimagine the possibilities of human psychological potential.

Chapter 23: Social Adaptation

23.1 Navigating Social Complexities

The social landscape was never a simple terrain for Elena Rodriguez. It was a complex, multidimensional ecosystem of psychological navigation, strategic interaction, and continuous transformation.

Her approach to social complexity emerged from the intricate survival strategies of her immigrant family—a deep understanding that social adaptation was not about conformity, but about creating sophisticated frameworks of mutual understanding and collective potential.

Carlos Rodriguez had been her first mentor of social strategy. "Social interactions," he would say, drawing intricate diagrams that blended sociological insight with engineering precision, "are not just exchanges. They are complex systems of mutual information and potential."

The technological platforms Elena developed were far more than social networking tools. They were comprehensive frameworks of social possibility—adaptive systems that could recognize complex social dynamics and create personalized strategies for meaningful social interaction and collective growth.

Her relationship with Gabriel Santos provided a unique collaborative lens for understanding social complexity. They didn't just navigate social spaces; they created collaborative ecosystems of social potential, challenging traditional notions of interpersonal connection.

Rosa Martinez, her longtime mentor, recognized the extraordinary depth of Elena's social exploration. "You're not just analyzing social interactions," Rosa would observe during their profound conversations. "You're systematically deconstructing and reimagining entire social landscapes."

Each social challenge became a site of profound research. Not in a clinical, detached sense, but as a genuine exploration of human social potential. Elena understood that social adaptation was never about achieving a fixed state of social acceptance. It was about creating expansive spaces of continuous learning and transformation.

Her work challenged traditional notions of social intelligence. Social complexities were not simply problems to be solved, but sophisticated information systems that offered profound insights into human potential for connection and understanding.

The international research collaborations that took her across different cultural landscapes were more than professional opportunities. They were comprehensive explorations of social boundaries, cultural adaptation, and the intricate dynamics of human interaction.

Her approach was fundamentally revolutionary. Social adaptation was not about fitting in, but about creating new frameworks of collective understanding and potential.

23.2 Adapting to Changing Environments

Social flexibility was never a simple process of adjustment for Elena Rodriguez. It was a complex, adaptive strategy of recognition, interpretation, and creative reimagination of social dynamics.

Her technological background provided a unique lens for understanding social complexity. She approached social adaptation with the same systematic curiosity she applied to complex technological systems. Each social interaction became a dataset, each cultural encounter a system waiting to be understood and expanded.

Marcus, her research collaborator, was fascinated by her approach. "You're developing a comprehensive framework of social evolution," he observed. "Not just navigating social spaces, but creating entire ecosystems of social potential."

Elena developed what she called a "social adaptation framework"—a comprehensive approach to understanding and transforming social interactions. The framework had multiple sophisticated components:

1. **Social Topology**: Mapping complex social landscapes
2. **Cultural Translation Mechanisms**: Identifying and interpreting social patterns
3. **Transformative Interaction Strategies**: Developing approaches to meaningful social connection

Her conversations with Gabriel became profound explorations of social potential. They didn't just discuss social adaptation. They created comprehensive models of how human beings could transform social challenges into sites of collective understanding and growth.

"Social flexibility," Gabriel would argue, "is often just poorly understood systems of human connectivity."

The technological tools Elena developed were extraordinary. Adaptive social assessment platforms that could recognize complex patterns of social interaction, that could create personalized strategies for navigating diverse social environments.

But these were never just about technological solutions. They were always about human potential, about creating broader pathways of social understanding and collective innovation.

Her work began to attract international attention. Sociologists, anthropologists, and cross-cultural communication experts all recognized that she was developing something far more profound than traditional social adaptation methodologies. She was creating a comprehensive approach to understanding human social potential.

The Rodriguez family's immigrant background provided a crucial contextual framework. Generations had navigated complex social landscapes, understanding that true social mastery was about survival, collective understanding, and continuous adaptation.

International conferences and research collaborations became sites of extraordinary social exploration. Elena wasn't just studying social dynamics; she was creating comprehensive dialogues about the future of human connection and cultural understanding.

23.3 The Art of Social Survival

The art of social survival was never about simple survival for Elena Rodriguez. It was a sophisticated ecosystem of social potential—a continuous process of reimagining social understanding that extended far beyond traditional notions of interpersonal interaction.

Her approach to social survival challenged every conventional narrative of human connection. Where traditional approaches saw social interactions as transactional encounters, Elena saw them as complex, adaptive systems offering profound insights into human potential.

The technological platforms she developed merged sophisticated machine learning algorithms with deep sociological and psychological insights. These weren't just social interaction tools. They were comprehensive ecosystems of social potential—platforms that could recognize complex social patterns and create transformative strategies for meaningful human connection.

"Social survival," she would explain to her research team, "is about developing the capacity to create relational possibilities where others see only limitations."

Her mother Maria's wisdom echoed in these moments of profound social exploration. "True social connection," Maria would say, "is not about fitting in. It's about creating space for collective understanding and growth."

Rosa Martinez observed this transformation with profound appreciation. "You're not just analyzing social interactions," Rosa would tell her. "You're creating entire new ecosystems of social possibility."

Elena's work demonstrated that social survival was a sophisticated form of collective imagination. Each social challenge became an opportunity for deeper understanding, for more nuanced interpersonal and cultural integration.

The boundaries between personal growth, technological innovation, and social understanding became increasingly fluid. Elena Rodriguez was not just a researcher or a technologist. She was an architect of social possibility, continuously reimagining the very concept of human social potential.

Her platforms were never just about technological solutions. They were always about human potential, about creating broader pathways of social understanding and creative reimagination.

As social landscapes continued to shift and transform, Elena Rodriguez stood at their complex intersection—not as an observer, but as a creative force of continuous social exploration.

Her approach was fundamentally revolutionary. Social survival was not about achieving a fixed state of social acceptance. It was about creating comprehensive ecosystems of social potential, about developing broader pathways of continuous human and collective growth.

Interpersonal strategies, she was demonstrating, were never a destination. They were always a journey of endless, beautiful becoming—a continuous process of creating more expansive, more compassionate ways of understanding human social potential.

In the intricate dance of social exploration, Elena Rodriguez had discovered something profound: that true social survival was not about perfect social navigation. It was about creating spaces of mutual understanding, about developing the capacity to grow, to learn, and to continuously reimagine the possibilities of human social potential.

Chapter 24: Romantic Evolution

24.1 Transforming Romantic Perspectives

Love was never a static concept for Elena Rodriguez. It was a dynamic, continuously evolving ecosystem of emotional and psychological potential—a sophisticated intersection of personal growth, technological innovation, and profound human connection.

Her approach to romantic relationships emerged from the intricate emotional landscapes cultivated by generations of Rodriguez family resilience. Love was not a destination to be reached, but a continuous journey of mutual transformation and collective potential.

Carlos Rodriguez had been her first mentor of emotional strategy. "Romantic connections," he would say, drawing intricate diagrams that blended emotional insight with engineering precision, "are complex adaptive systems of human potential."

The technological platforms Elena developed were far more than relationship assessment tools. They were comprehensive frameworks of romantic possibility—adaptive systems that could recognize complex emotional dynamics and create personalized strategies for meaningful, transformative romantic connections.

Her relationship with Gabriel Santos represented the living embodiment of this philosophical approach. They weren't just romantic partners; they were collaborative architects of emotional potential, continuously reimagining the boundaries of intimate connection.

Rosa Martinez, her longtime mentor, recognized the extraordinary depth of Elena's romantic exploration. "You're not just analyzing relationships," Rosa would observe during their profound conversations. "You're systematically deconstructing and reimagining entire emotional ecosystems."

Each romantic challenge became a site of profound research. Not in a clinical, detached sense, but as a genuine exploration of human emotional potential. Elena understood that romantic evolution was never about achieving a fixed state of relationship stability. It was about creating expansive spaces of continuous learning and emotional transformation.

Her work challenged traditional notions of romantic development. Romantic perspectives were not simply fixed emotional states to be maintained, but sophisticated information systems that offered profound insights into human potential for connection.

The international experiences that shaped her relationship with Gabriel were more than geographic challenges. They were comprehensive explorations of emotional boundaries, cultural adaptation, and the intricate dynamics of intimate human connection.

Her approach was fundamentally revolutionary. Romantic evolution was not about finding the perfect partner, but about creating new frameworks of mutual understanding and emotional potential.

24.2 Navigating Emotional Complexities

Emotional complexity was never a simple terrain for Elena Rodriguez. It was a complex, adaptive strategy of emotional recognition, interpretation, and creative reimagination of romantic dynamics.

Her technological background provided a unique lens for understanding the intricate landscapes of romantic connection. She approached romantic challenges with the same systematic curiosity she applied to complex technological systems. Each emotional interaction became a dataset, each intimate encounter a system waiting to be understood and expanded.

Marcus, her research collaborator, was fascinated by her approach. "You're developing a comprehensive framework of romantic evolution," he observed. "Not just navigating emotional spaces, but creating entire ecosystems of intimate potential."

Elena developed what she called a "romantic liberation framework"—a comprehensive approach to understanding and transforming intimate connections. The framework had multiple sophisticated components:

1. **Emotional Topology**: Mapping complex romantic landscapes
2. **Intimacy Translation Mechanisms**: Identifying and interpreting emotional patterns
3. **Transformative Connection Strategies**: Developing approaches to meaningful romantic growth

Her conversations with Gabriel became profound explorations of emotional potential. They didn't just discuss romantic challenges. They created comprehensive models of how human beings could transform intimate encounters into sites of collective emotional growth.

"Romantic complexity," Gabriel would argue, "is often just poorly understood systems of human emotional connectivity."

The technological tools Elena developed were extraordinary. Adaptive emotional assessment platforms that could recognize complex patterns of romantic interaction, that could create personalized strategies for navigating the most intricate emotional landscapes.

But these were never just about technological solutions. They were always about human potential, about creating broader pathways of emotional understanding and collective intimate innovation.

Her work began to attract international attention. Relationship experts, psychologists, and cultural anthropologists all recognized that she was developing something far more profound than traditional relationship methodologies. She was creating a comprehensive approach to understanding human romantic potential.

The Rodriguez family's emotional resilience provided a crucial contextual framework. Generations had navigated complex romantic landscapes, understanding that true intimate mastery was about survival, collective understanding, and continuous emotional adaptation.

International collaborations and shared experiences became sites of extraordinary romantic exploration. Elena wasn't just studying romantic dynamics; she was creating comprehensive dialogues about the future of human connection and emotional potential.

24.3 Love as a Catalyst for Change

Love was never a passive experience for Elena Rodriguez. It was a sophisticated ecosystem of emotional potential—a continuous process of reimagining romantic understanding that extended far beyond traditional notions of intimate connection.

Her approach to love challenged every conventional narrative of romantic development. Where traditional approaches saw relationships as static entities,

Elena saw them as complex, adaptive systems offering profound insights into human potential for emotional transformation.

The technological platforms she developed merged sophisticated machine learning algorithms with deep psychological and emotional insights. These weren't just relationship tools. They were comprehensive ecosystems of romantic potential—platforms that could recognize complex emotional patterns and create transformative strategies for meaningful human connection.

"Love," she would explain to her research team, "is about developing the capacity to create emotional possibilities where others see only limitations."

Her mother Maria's wisdom echoed in these moments of profound romantic exploration. "True intimate connection," Maria would say, "is not about possession. It's about creating space for collective emotional growth and individual transformation."

Rosa Martinez observed this transformation with profound appreciation. "You're not just analyzing romantic interactions," Rosa would tell her. "You're creating entire new ecosystems of emotional possibility."

Elena's work demonstrated that love was a sophisticated form of collective imagination. Each romantic challenge became an opportunity for deeper understanding, for more nuanced emotional and personal integration.

The boundaries between personal growth, technological innovation, and emotional understanding became increasingly fluid. Elena Rodriguez was not just a researcher or a technologist. She was an architect of romantic possibility, continuously reimagining the very concept of human emotional potential.

Her platforms were never just about technological solutions. They were always about human potential, about creating broader pathways of emotional understanding and creative reimagination.

As romantic landscapes continued to shift and transform, Elena Rodriguez stood at their complex intersection—not as an observer, but as a creative force of continuous emotional exploration.

Her approach was fundamentally revolutionary. Love was not about achieving a fixed state of romantic stability. It was about creating comprehensive ecosystems of emotional potential, about developing broader pathways of continuous human and emotional growth.

Romantic transformation, she was demonstrating, was never a destination. It was always a journey of endless, beautiful becoming—a continuous process of creating more expansive, more compassionate ways of understanding human emotional potential.

In the intricate dance of romantic exploration, Elena Rodriguez had discovered something profound: that true love was not about perfect emotional connection. It was about creating spaces of mutual understanding, about developing the capacity to grow, to learn, and to continuously reimagine the possibilities of human emotional potential.

Chapter 25: Economic Empowerment

25.1 Financial Self-Determination

Economic potential was never a simple calculation for Elena Rodriguez. It was a complex, multidimensional ecosystem of psychological, technological, and strategic possibility—a sophisticated intersection of personal ambition, family legacy, and collective transformation.

Her approach to economic empowerment emerged from the intricate survival strategies of her immigrant family—a deep understanding that financial independence was not about accumulating wealth, but about creating comprehensive frameworks of economic potential and personal liberation.

Carlos Rodriguez had been her first mentor of economic strategy. "Wealth," he would say, drawing intricate diagrams that blended financial insight with philosophical precision, "is not just about money. It's about creating systems of possibility."

The technological platforms Elena developed were far more than financial assessment tools. They were comprehensive frameworks of economic potential—adaptive systems that could recognize complex economic dynamics and create personalized strategies for meaningful financial growth and personal empowerment.

Her collaboration with Gabriel Santos provided a unique lens for understanding economic complexity. They didn't just analyze financial systems; they created collaborative ecosystems of economic potential, challenging traditional notions of wealth and value.

Rosa Martinez, her longtime mentor, recognized the extraordinary depth of Elena's economic exploration. "You're not just analyzing financial patterns," Rosa would observe during their profound conversations. "You're systematically deconstructing and reimagining entire economic landscapes."

Each economic challenge became a site of profound research. Not in a clinical, detached sense, but as a genuine exploration of human economic potential. Elena understood that financial self-determination was never about achieving a fixed state of monetary success. It was about creating expansive spaces of continuous learning and economic transformation.

Her work challenged traditional notions of economic independence. Financial potential was not simply a matter of individual achievement, but a sophisticated information system that offered profound insights into human potential for collective economic growth.

The international research collaborations that explored economic innovation were more than academic pursuits. They were comprehensive explorations of economic boundaries, technological potential, and the intricate dynamics of financial empowerment.

Her approach was fundamentally revolutionary. Economic independence was not about individual accumulation, but about creating new frameworks of collective economic potential and personal liberation.

25.2 Strategies for Economic Advancement

Economic strategy was never a simple process of financial calculation for Elena Rodriguez. It was a complex, adaptive strategy of economic recognition, technological innovation, and creative reimagination of financial dynamics.

Her technological background provided a unique lens for understanding the intricate landscapes of economic potential. She approached financial growth with the same systematic curiosity she applied to complex technological systems. Each economic interaction became a dataset, each financial encounter a system waiting to be understood and expanded.

Marcus, her research collaborator, was fascinated by her approach. "You're developing a comprehensive framework of economic evolution," he observed. "Not just navigating financial spaces, but creating entire ecosystems of economic potential."

Elena developed what she called an "economic liberation framework"—a comprehensive approach to understanding and transforming economic potential. The framework had multiple sophisticated components:

1. **Economic Topology**: Mapping complex financial landscapes
2. **Value Translation Mechanisms**: Identifying and interpreting economic patterns
3. **Transformative Economic Strategies**: Developing approaches to meaningful financial growth

Her conversations with Gabriel became profound explorations of economic potential. They didn't just discuss financial strategies. They created comprehensive models of how human beings could transform economic challenges into sites of collective financial innovation.

"Economic advancement," Gabriel would argue, "is often just poorly understood systems of human economic capability."

The technological tools Elena developed were extraordinary. Adaptive economic assessment platforms that could recognize complex patterns of financial interaction, that could create personalized strategies for navigating the most intricate economic landscapes.

But these were never just about technological solutions. They were always about human potential, about creating broader pathways of economic understanding and collective financial innovation.

Her work began to attract international attention. Economists, financial strategists, and social innovation experts all recognized that she was developing something far more profound than traditional economic methodologies. She was creating a comprehensive approach to understanding human economic potential.

The Rodriguez family's economic resilience provided a crucial contextual framework. Generations had navigated complex economic landscapes, understanding that true financial mastery was about survival, collective understanding, and continuous economic adaptation.

International collaborations and research initiatives became sites of extraordinary economic exploration. Elena wasn't just studying financial dynamics; she was creating comprehensive dialogues about the future of economic potential and human empowerment.

25.3 Wealth as Personal Empowerment

Wealth was never a passive concept for Elena Rodriguez. It was a sophisticated ecosystem of economic potential—a continuous process of reimagining economic understanding that extended far beyond traditional notions of financial success.

Her approach to economic potential challenged every conventional narrative of wealth creation. Where traditional approaches saw financial growth as an individual pursuit, Elena saw it as a complex, adaptive system offering profound insights into human potential for collective economic transformation.

The technological platforms she developed merged sophisticated machine learning algorithms with deep economic and sociological insights. These weren't just financial tools. They were comprehensive ecosystems of economic potential—platforms that could recognize complex economic patterns and create transformative strategies for meaningful economic empowerment.

"Economic potential," she would explain to her research team, "is about developing the capacity to create financial possibilities where others see only limitations."

Her mother Maria's wisdom echoed in these moments of profound economic exploration. "True wealth," Maria would say, "is not about accumulation. It's about creating space for collective economic growth and individual liberation."

Rosa Martinez observed this transformation with profound appreciation. "You're not just analyzing financial interactions," Rosa would tell her. "You're creating entire new ecosystems of economic possibility."

Elena's work demonstrated that wealth was a sophisticated form of collective imagination. Each economic challenge became an opportunity for deeper understanding, for more nuanced economic and personal integration.

The boundaries between personal growth, technological innovation, and economic understanding became increasingly fluid. Elena Rodriguez was not just a researcher or a technologist. She was an architect of economic possibility, continuously reimagining the very concept of human economic potential.

Her platforms were never just about technological solutions. They were always about human potential, about creating broader pathways of economic understanding and creative reimagination.

As economic landscapes continued to shift and transform, Elena Rodriguez stood at their complex intersection—not as an observer, but as a creative force of continuous economic exploration.

Her approach was fundamentally revolutionary. Wealth was not about achieving a fixed state of financial success. It was about creating comprehensive ecosystems of economic potential, about developing broader pathways of continuous human and economic growth.

Economic empowerment, she was demonstrating, was never a destination. It was always a journey of endless, beautiful becoming—a continuous process of creating more expansive, more compassionate ways of understanding human economic potential.

In the intricate dance of economic exploration, Elena Rodriguez had discovered something profound: that true wealth was not about individual financial accumulation. It was about creating spaces of mutual economic understanding, about developing the capacity to grow, to learn, and to continuously reimagine the possibilities of human economic potential.

Chapter 26: Ethical Evolution

26.1 Developing Moral Complexity

Ethical understanding was never a simple binary of right and wrong for Elena Rodriguez. It was a complex, multidimensional ecosystem of moral possibility—a sophisticated intersection of personal integrity, technological innovation, and profound human potential.

Her approach to ethical complexity emerged from the intricate moral landscapes cultivated by generations of Rodriguez family resilience. Morality was not a fixed set of rules to be followed, but a continuously evolving process of understanding, challenging, and reimagining human potential.

Carlos Rodriguez had been her first mentor of ethical strategy. "Moral understanding," he would say, drawing intricate diagrams that blended philosophical insight with engineering precision, "is a dynamic system of collective human potential."

The technological platforms Elena developed were far more than ethical assessment tools. They were comprehensive frameworks of moral possibility—adaptive systems that could recognize complex ethical dynamics and create personalized strategies for meaningful moral growth and collective understanding.

Her collaboration with Gabriel Santos provided a unique lens for understanding ethical complexity. They didn't just analyze moral challenges; they created collaborative ecosystems of ethical potential, challenging traditional notions of right and wrong.

Rosa Martinez, her longtime mentor, recognized the extraordinary depth of Elena's ethical exploration. "You're not just analyzing moral patterns," Rosa would observe during their profound conversations. "You're systematically deconstructing and reimagining entire ethical landscapes."

Each moral challenge became a site of profound research. Not in a clinical, detached sense, but as a genuine exploration of human ethical potential. Elena understood that ethical maturation was never about achieving a fixed state of moral perfection. It was about creating expansive spaces of continuous learning and ethical transformation.

Her work challenged traditional notions of moral development. Ethical complexity was not simply a matter of following predetermined rules, but a sophisticated information system that offered profound insights into human potential for collective moral growth.

The international research collaborations that explored ethical innovation were more than academic pursuits. They were comprehensive explorations of moral boundaries, technological potential, and the intricate dynamics of human ethical understanding.

Her approach was fundamentally revolutionary. Ethical evolution was not about achieving moral certainty, but about creating new frameworks of collective moral potential and individual ethical liberation.

26.2 Navigating Moral Ambiguities

Moral navigation was never a simple process of ethical calculation for Elena Rodriguez. It was a complex, adaptive strategy of ethical recognition, philosophical innovation, and creative reimagination of moral dynamics.

Her technological background provided a unique lens for understanding the intricate landscapes of ethical potential. She approached moral challenges with the same systematic curiosity she applied to complex technological systems. Each ethical interaction became a dataset, each moral encounter a system waiting to be understood and expanded.

Marcus, her research collaborator, was fascinated by her approach. "You're developing a comprehensive framework of ethical evolution," he observed. "Not just navigating moral spaces, but creating entire ecosystems of ethical potential."

Elena developed what she called an "ethical liberation framework"—a comprehensive approach to understanding and transforming moral potential. The framework had multiple sophisticated components:

1. **Ethical Topology**: Mapping complex moral landscapes
2. **Moral Translation Mechanisms**: Identifying and interpreting ethical patterns
3. **Transformative Ethical Strategies**: Developing approaches to meaningful moral growth

Her conversations with Gabriel became profound explorations of ethical potential. They didn't just discuss moral challenges. They created comprehensive models of how human beings could transform ethical dilemmas into sites of collective moral innovation.

"Moral ambiguity," Gabriel would argue, "is often just poorly understood systems of human ethical capability."

The technological tools Elena developed were extraordinary. Adaptive ethical assessment platforms that could recognize complex patterns of moral interaction, that could create personalized strategies for navigating the most intricate ethical landscapes.

But these were never just about technological solutions. They were always about human potential, about creating broader pathways of ethical understanding and collective moral innovation.

Her work began to attract international attention. Philosophers, ethicists, and social innovation experts all recognized that she was developing something far more profound than traditional moral methodologies. She was creating a comprehensive approach to understanding human ethical potential.

The Rodriguez family's moral resilience provided a crucial contextual framework. Generations had navigated complex ethical landscapes, understanding that true moral mastery was about survival, collective understanding, and continuous ethical adaptation.

International collaborations and research initiatives became sites of extraordinary ethical exploration. Elena wasn't just studying moral dynamics; she was creating comprehensive dialogues about the future of ethical potential and human empowerment.

26.3 The Refinement of Ethical Understanding

Ethical understanding was never a passive concept for Elena Rodriguez. It was a sophisticated ecosystem of moral potential—a continuous process of reimagining ethical understanding that extended far beyond traditional notions of moral development.

Her approach to ethical potential challenged every conventional narrative of moral growth. Where traditional approaches saw ethics as a fixed set of principles, Elena saw them as complex, adaptive systems offering profound insights into human potential for moral transformation.

The technological platforms she developed merged sophisticated machine learning algorithms with deep philosophical and sociological insights. These weren't just ethical assessment tools. They were comprehensive ecosystems of moral potential—platforms that could recognize complex ethical patterns and create transformative strategies for meaningful moral growth.

"Ethical understanding," she would explain to her research team, "is about developing the capacity to create moral possibilities where others see only limitations."

Her mother Maria's wisdom echoed in these moments of profound ethical exploration. "True moral growth," Maria would say, "is not about rigid adherence to rules. It's about creating space for collective ethical evolution and individual moral liberation."

Rosa Martinez observed this transformation with profound appreciation. "You're not just analyzing ethical interactions," Rosa would tell her. "You're creating entire new ecosystems of moral possibility."

Elena's work demonstrated that ethical understanding was a sophisticated form of collective imagination. Each moral challenge became an opportunity for deeper understanding, for more nuanced ethical and personal integration.

The boundaries between personal growth, technological innovation, and ethical understanding became increasingly fluid. Elena Rodriguez was not just a researcher or a technologist. She was an architect of moral possibility, continuously reimagining the very concept of human ethical potential.

Her platforms were never just about technological solutions. They were always about human potential, about creating broader pathways of ethical understanding and creative reimagination.

As ethical landscapes continued to shift and transform, Elena Rodriguez stood at their complex intersection—not as an observer, but as a creative force of continuous ethical exploration.

Her approach was fundamentally revolutionary. Ethical understanding was not about achieving a fixed state of moral certainty. It was about creating comprehensive ecosystems of moral potential, about developing broader pathways of continuous human and ethical growth.

Moral refinement, she was demonstrating, was never a destination. It was always a journey of endless, beautiful becoming—a continuous process of creating more expansive, more compassionate ways of understanding human ethical potential.

In the intricate dance of ethical exploration, Elena Rodriguez had discovered something profound: that true moral growth was not about perfect ethical adherence. It was about creating spaces of mutual ethical understanding, about developing the capacity to grow, to learn, and to continuously reimagine the possibilities of human moral potential.

Chapter 27: Intellectual Exploration

27.1 Expanding Intellectual Boundaries

Intellectual exploration was never a passive journey for Elena Rodriguez. It was a dynamic, transformative process of continuously challenging and reimagining the very boundaries of human knowledge. Where others saw limitations, she perceived infinite landscapes of potential understanding—intricate networks of interconnected insights waiting to be discovered, decoded, and reimagined.

Her approach to intellectual growth emerged from a profound family legacy of curiosity and resilience. The Rodriguez intellectual tradition was not about accumulating knowledge as a static collection of facts, but about creating living, breathing ecosystems of understanding—dynamic frameworks that could adapt, evolve, and transform.

Carlos Rodriguez, her father, had been her first intellectual mentor. "Knowledge is not a destination," he would tell her during their long conversations that blended scientific precision with philosophical depth. "It's a continuous journey of expansion, of challenging what we believe we understand."

The technological platforms Elena developed were far more than research tools. They were comprehensive intellectual exploration systems—adaptive frameworks that could recognize complex knowledge patterns, identify emergent connections, and create personalized strategies for intellectual growth and collective understanding.

Her collaboration with international research teams provided a unique lens for understanding intellectual boundaries. They didn't just analyze existing knowledge structures; they created collaborative ecosystems of intellectual potential, challenging traditional notions of disciplinary constraints and academic limitations.

Rosa Martinez, her longtime mentor, recognized the extraordinary depth of Elena's intellectual exploration. "You're not just analyzing knowledge patterns," Rosa would observe during their profound discussions. "You're systematically deconstructing and reimagining entire intellectual landscapes."

Each intellectual challenge became a site of profound research. Not in a clinical, detached sense, but as a genuine exploration of human cognitive potential. Elena understood that intellectual growth was never about achieving a fixed state of knowledge. It was about creating expansive spaces of continuous learning and intellectual transformation.

Her work challenged traditional academic paradigms. Intellectual exploration was not simply a matter of acquiring information, but a sophisticated information system that offered profound insights into human potential for collective cognitive growth.

The international research collaborations that explored intellectual innovation were more than academic pursuits. They were comprehensive explorations of knowledge boundaries, technological potential, and the intricate dynamics of human intellectual understanding.

Her approach was fundamentally revolutionary. Intellectual exploration was not about achieving intellectual certainty, but about creating new frameworks of collective cognitive potential and individual intellectual liberation.

27.2 Challenging Established Thinking

Intellectual rebellion was not a confrontational act for Elena Rodriguez. It was a sophisticated strategy of reimagining knowledge systems, of creating more expansive, more inclusive frameworks of understanding that could transcend traditional disciplinary boundaries.

Her technological background provided a unique lens for understanding the intricate landscapes of intellectual potential. She approached intellectual challenges with the same systematic curiosity she applied to complex technological systems. Each intellectual interaction became a dataset, each cognitive encounter a system waiting to be understood and expanded.

Marcus, her research collaborator, was fascinated by her approach. "You're developing a comprehensive framework of intellectual evolution," he observed. "Not just challenging existing knowledge, but creating entire ecosystems of intellectual potential."

Elena developed what she called an "intellectual liberation framework"—a comprehensive approach to understanding and transforming cognitive potential. The framework had multiple sophisticated components:

1. **Intellectual Topology**: Mapping complex knowledge landscapes
2. **Cognitive Translation Mechanisms**: Identifying and interpreting intellectual patterns
3. **Transformative Intellectual Strategies**: Developing approaches to meaningful cognitive growth

Her conversations with Gabriel became profound explorations of intellectual potential. They didn't just discuss academic challenges. They created comprehensive models of how human beings could transform intellectual barriers into sites of collective cognitive innovation.

"Intellectual limitations," Gabriel would argue, "are often just poorly understood systems of human cognitive capability."

The technological tools Elena developed were extraordinary. Adaptive intellectual assessment platforms that could recognize complex patterns of cognitive interaction, that could create personalized strategies for navigating the most intricate intellectual landscapes.

But these were never just about technological solutions. They were always about human potential, about creating broader pathways of intellectual understanding and collective cognitive innovation.

Her work began to attract international attention. Academics, researchers, and innovation experts all recognized that she was developing something far more profound than traditional academic methodologies. She was creating a comprehensive approach to understanding human intellectual potential.

The Rodriguez family's intellectual resilience provided a crucial contextual framework. Generations had navigated complex knowledge landscapes, understanding that true intellectual mastery was about survival, collective understanding, and continuous cognitive adaptation.

International collaborations and research initiatives became sites of extraordinary intellectual exploration. Elena wasn't just studying knowledge dynamics; she was creating comprehensive dialogues about the future of intellectual potential and human empowerment.

27.3 The Pursuit of Knowledge

Knowledge, for Elena Rodriguez, was never a static collection of information. It was a living, breathing ecosystem of intellectual potential—a continuous process of reimagining understanding that extended far beyond traditional notions of academic learning.

Her approach to intellectual potential challenged every conventional narrative of cognitive development. Where traditional approaches saw learning as a linear progression, Elena saw it as complex, adaptive systems offering profound insights into human potential for intellectual transformation.

The technological platforms she developed merged sophisticated machine learning algorithms with deep philosophical and sociological insights. These weren't just research tools. They were comprehensive ecosystems of intellectual potential—platforms that could recognize complex cognitive patterns and create transformative strategies for meaningful intellectual growth.

"Continuous learning," she would explain to her research team, "is about developing the capacity to create intellectual possibilities where others see only limitations."

Her mother Maria's wisdom echoed in these moments of profound intellectual exploration. "True learning," Maria would say, "is not about rigid adherence to existing knowledge. It's about creating space for collective intellectual evolution and individual cognitive liberation."

Rosa Martinez observed this transformation with profound appreciation. "You're not just analyzing intellectual interactions," Rosa would tell her. "You're creating entire new ecosystems of cognitive possibility."

Elena's work demonstrated that the pursuit of knowledge was a sophisticated form of collective imagination. Each intellectual challenge became an opportunity for deeper understanding, for more nuanced cognitive and personal integration.

The boundaries between personal growth, technological innovation, and intellectual understanding became increasingly fluid. Elena Rodriguez was not just a researcher or a technologist. She was an architect of cognitive possibility, continuously reimagining the very concept of human intellectual potential.

Her platforms were never just about technological solutions. They were always about human potential, about creating broader pathways of intellectual understanding and creative reimagination.

As intellectual landscapes continued to shift and transform, Elena Rodriguez stood at their complex intersection—not as an observer, but as a creative force of continuous intellectual exploration.

Her approach was fundamentally revolutionary. The pursuit of knowledge was not about achieving a fixed state of intellectual certainty. It was about creating comprehensive ecosystems of cognitive potential, about developing broader pathways of continuous human and intellectual growth.

Knowledge refinement, she was demonstrating, was never a destination. It was always a journey of endless, beautiful becoming—a continuous process of creating more expansive, more nuanced ways of understanding human intellectual potential.

In the intricate dance of intellectual exploration, Elena Rodriguez had discovered something profound: that true learning was not about perfect knowledge acquisition. It was about creating spaces of mutual intellectual understanding, about developing the capacity to grow, to learn, and to continuously reimagine the possibilities of human cognitive potential.

Chapter 28: Personal Transformation

28.1 Redefining Personal Potential

Personal transformation was never a linear journey for Elena Rodriguez. It was a complex, multidimensional process of continuous reimagination—an intricate dance of self-discovery that defied traditional narratives of personal growth and individual potential.

Her approach to self-reinvention emerged from a profound understanding that human potential was not a fixed state, but a dynamic ecosystem of possibility. Each moment of personal challenge became an opportunity for radical reimagination, a chance to deconstruct and reconstruct the very essence of her identity.

The Rodriguez family legacy of resilience provided a powerful foundation for this transformative journey. Generations had understood that true personal growth was not about conforming to external expectations, but about creating expansive spaces of individual potential and collective understanding.

Carlos Rodriguez, her father, had been her first mentor of personal transformation. "Identity is not a static construct," he would tell her during their profound conversations. "It's a continuous process of becoming—a dynamic system of potential waiting to be explored and expanded."

The technological platforms Elena developed were far more than personal development tools. They were comprehensive frameworks of self-reinvention—adaptive systems that could recognize complex personal patterns, identify transformative opportunities, and create personalized strategies for meaningful personal growth.

Her collaboration with psychological researchers and innovation experts provided a unique lens for understanding personal transformation. They didn't just analyze individual growth; they created collaborative ecosystems of personal potential, challenging traditional notions of human limitation and individual capacity.

Rosa Martinez, her longtime mentor, recognized the extraordinary depth of Elena's personal exploration. "You're not just analyzing personal patterns,"

Rosa would observe during their intimate discussions. "You're systematically deconstructing and reimagining entire landscapes of human potential."

Each personal challenge became a site of profound research. Not in a clinical, detached sense, but as a genuine exploration of human capacity for radical self-reinvention. Elena understood that personal transformation was never about achieving a fixed state of perfection. It was about creating expansive spaces of continuous learning and individual evolution.

Her work challenged traditional psychological paradigms. Personal potential was not simply a matter of incremental improvement, but a sophisticated system that offered profound insights into human capacity for comprehensive self-transformation.

The international collaborations that explored personal innovation were more than academic pursuits. They were comprehensive explorations of human potential, technological innovation, and the intricate dynamics of individual growth and collective understanding.

Her approach was fundamentally revolutionary. Personal transformation was not about achieving a predetermined version of self, but about creating new frameworks of individual potential and personal liberation.

28.2 Breaking Personal Limitations

Personal liberation was not a singular moment of breakthrough for Elena Rodriguez. It was a sophisticated strategy of systematically dismantling internal and external constraints, of creating more expansive, more authentic frameworks of individual existence.

Her technological and psychological background provided a unique lens for understanding the intricate landscapes of personal potential. She approached personal limitations with the same systematic curiosity she applied to complex technological and cognitive systems. Each personal challenge became a dataset, each internal constraint a system waiting to be understood and transcended.

Marcus, her research collaborator, was fascinated by her approach. "You're developing a comprehensive framework of personal evolution," he observed. "Not just breaking limitations, but creating entire ecosystems of individual potential."

Elena developed what she called a "personal liberation framework"—a comprehensive approach to understanding and transforming individual potential. The framework had multiple sophisticated components:

1. **Personal Topology**: Mapping complex internal landscapes
2. **Constraint Translation Mechanisms**: Identifying and interpreting personal limitations
3. **Transformative Personal Strategies**: Developing approaches to meaningful individual growth

Her conversations with Gabriel became profound explorations of personal potential. They didn't just discuss personal challenges. They created comprehensive models of how human beings could transform internal barriers into sites of radical personal innovation.

"Personal limitations," Gabriel would argue, "are often just poorly understood systems of human potential waiting to be reimagined."

The technological tools Elena developed were extraordinary. Adaptive personal assessment platforms that could recognize complex patterns of internal constraint, that could create personalized strategies for navigating the most intricate personal landscapes.

But these were never just about technological solutions. They were always about human potential, about creating broader pathways of personal understanding and individual liberation.

Her work began to attract international attention. Psychologists, philosophers, and innovation experts all recognized that she was developing something far more profound than traditional personal development methodologies. She was creating a comprehensive approach to understanding human potential for radical self-transformation.

The Rodriguez family's resilience provided a crucial contextual framework. Generations had navigated complex personal landscapes, understanding that true personal liberation was about survival, collective understanding, and continuous individual adaptation.

International collaborations and research initiatives became sites of extraordinary personal exploration. Elena wasn't just studying personal dynamics; she was creating comprehensive dialogues about the future of individual potential and human empowerment.

28.3 The Journey of Self-Actualization

Self-actualization, for Elena Rodriguez, was never a destination to be reached. It was a living, breathing ecosystem of personal potential—a continuous process of reimagining individual existence that extended far beyond traditional notions of personal development.

Her approach to personal potential challenged every conventional narrative of individual growth. Where traditional approaches saw self-actualization as a linear progression, Elena saw it as complex, adaptive systems offering profound insights into human capacity for comprehensive transformation.

The technological platforms she developed merged sophisticated psychological assessment algorithms with deep philosophical and sociological insights. These weren't just personal development tools. They were comprehensive ecosystems of individual potential—platforms that could recognize complex personal patterns and create transformative strategies for meaningful personal growth.

"Self-actualization," she would explain to her research team, "is about developing the capacity to create personal possibilities where others see only limitations."

Her mother Maria's wisdom echoed in these moments of profound personal exploration. "True personal growth," Maria would say, "is not about achieving a predetermined version of self. It's about creating space for individual evolution and personal liberation."

Rosa Martinez observed this transformation with profound appreciation. "You're not just analyzing personal interactions," Rosa would tell her. "You're creating entire new ecosystems of individual possibility."

Elena's work demonstrated that self-actualization was a sophisticated form of collective and individual imagination. Each personal challenge became an opportunity for deeper understanding, for more nuanced personal and collective integration.

The boundaries between personal growth, technological innovation, and psychological understanding became increasingly fluid. Elena Rodriguez was not just a researcher or a technologist. She was an architect of personal possibility, continuously reimagining the very concept of human potential for self-transformation.

Her platforms were never just about technological solutions. They were always about human potential, about creating broader pathways of personal understanding and creative reimagination.

As personal landscapes continued to shift and transform, Elena Rodriguez stood at their complex intersection—not as an observer, but as a creative force of continuous personal exploration.

Her approach was fundamentally revolutionary. The journey of self-actualization was not about achieving a fixed state of personal perfection. It was about creating comprehensive ecosystems of individual potential, about developing broader pathways of continuous human and personal growth.

Personal refinement, she was demonstrating, was never a destination. It was always a journey of endless, beautiful becoming—a continuous process of creating more expansive, more authentic ways of understanding human potential for individual transformation.

In the intricate dance of personal exploration, Elena Rodriguez had discovered something profound: that true self-actualization was not about perfect self-realization. It was about creating spaces of mutual understanding, about developing the capacity to grow, to learn, and to continuously reimagine the possibilities of human individual potential.

Chapter 29: Romantic Resilience

29.1 Overcoming Romantic Challenges

Romantic resilience was never a simple matter of endurance for Elena Rodriguez. It was a sophisticated ecosystem of emotional intelligence, strategic understanding, and profound human connection—a complex interplay of personal growth and intimate relationship dynamics that transcended traditional narratives of love and partnership.

Her approach to romantic challenges emerged from a deep familial legacy of emotional wisdom and relational complexity. The Rodriguez family understood love not as a passive experience, but as an active, transformative journey of mutual growth and collective emotional intelligence.

Carlos and Maria Rodriguez had modeled a unique approach to romantic resilience. "Love is not about finding the perfect person," her father would say during family conversations that blended philosophical insight with emotional depth. "It's about creating a shared ecosystem of mutual understanding and continuous personal growth."

The technological and psychological platforms Elena developed were far more than relationship assessment tools. They were comprehensive frameworks of romantic potential—adaptive systems that could recognize complex emotional patterns, identify transformative relationship opportunities, and create personalized strategies for meaningful romantic connection and individual empowerment.

Her collaboration with relationship experts and psychological researchers provided a unique lens for understanding romantic challenges. They didn't just analyze relationship dynamics; they created collaborative ecosystems of romantic potential, challenging traditional notions of love, partnership, and emotional connection.

Rosa Martinez, her longtime mentor, recognized the extraordinary depth of Elena's romantic exploration. "You're not just analyzing relationship patterns," Rosa would observe during their profound discussions. "You're systematically deconstructing and reimagining entire landscapes of romantic potential."

Each romantic challenge became a site of profound research. Not in a clinical, detached sense, but as a genuine exploration of human capacity for deep, transformative emotional connection. Elena understood that romantic resilience was never about achieving a fixed state of relationship perfection. It was about creating expansive spaces of continuous learning, emotional growth, and mutual understanding.

Her work challenged traditional psychological and sociological paradigms of love. Romantic resilience was not simply a matter of overcoming obstacles, but a sophisticated information system that offered profound insights into human potential for deep, meaningful emotional connection.

The international research collaborations that explored romantic innovation were more than academic pursuits. They were comprehensive explorations of emotional boundaries, personal potential, and the intricate dynamics of human romantic understanding.

Her approach was fundamentally revolutionary. Romantic resilience was not about achieving relationship certainty, but about creating new frameworks of collective emotional potential and individual romantic liberation.

29.2 Navigating Emotional Complexities

Emotional navigation was not a linear journey for Elena Rodriguez. It was a sophisticated strategy of understanding the intricate landscapes of romantic connection, of creating more expansive, more authentic frameworks of intimate relationship dynamics.

Her technological and psychological background provided a unique lens for understanding the complex terrains of romantic potential. She approached emotional challenges with the same systematic curiosity she applied to complex technological and cognitive systems. Each romantic interaction became a dataset, each emotional encounter a system waiting to be understood and expanded.

Marcus, her research collaborator, was fascinated by her approach. "You're developing a comprehensive framework of romantic evolution," he observed. "Not just navigating emotional challenges, but creating entire ecosystems of romantic potential."

Elena developed what she called a "romantic navigation framework"—a comprehensive approach to understanding and transforming intimate relationship potential. The framework had multiple sophisticated components:

1. **Emotional Topology**: Mapping complex romantic landscapes
2. **Intimacy Translation Mechanisms**: Identifying and interpreting emotional patterns
3. **Transformative Relationship Strategies**: Developing approaches to meaningful romantic growth

Her conversations with Gabriel became profound explorations of romantic potential. They didn't just discuss relationship challenges. They created comprehensive models of how human beings could transform emotional barriers into sites of radical romantic innovation.

"Romantic limitations," Gabriel would argue, "are often just poorly understood systems of human emotional capability waiting to be reimagined."

The technological tools Elena developed were extraordinary. Adaptive emotional assessment platforms that could recognize complex patterns of romantic interaction, that could create personalized strategies for navigating the most intricate emotional landscapes.

But these were never just about technological solutions. They were always about human potential, about creating broader pathways of emotional understanding and romantic liberation.

Her work began to attract international attention. Relationship experts, psychologists, and social innovators all recognized that she was developing something far more profound than traditional relationship methodologies. She was creating a comprehensive approach to understanding human potential for deep, transformative romantic connection.

The Rodriguez family's emotional resilience provided a crucial contextual framework. Generations had navigated complex romantic landscapes, understanding that true romantic endurance was about survival, collective understanding, and continuous emotional adaptation.

International collaborations and research initiatives became sites of extraordinary romantic exploration. Elena wasn't just studying relationship dynamics; she was creating comprehensive dialogues about the future of romantic potential and human emotional empowerment.

29.3 Love as a Source of Strength

Love, for Elena Rodriguez, was never a passive emotional state. It was a living, breathing ecosystem of emotional potential—a continuous process of reimagining intimate connection that extended far beyond traditional notions of romantic relationships.

Her approach to romantic potential challenged every conventional narrative of emotional development. Where traditional approaches saw love as a static experience, Elena saw it as complex, adaptive systems offering profound insights into human capacity for comprehensive emotional transformation.

The technological platforms she developed merged sophisticated emotional intelligence algorithms with deep philosophical and sociological insights. These weren't just relationship tools. They were comprehensive ecosystems of romantic potential—platforms that could recognize complex emotional patterns and create transformative strategies for meaningful romantic growth.

"Emotional resilience," she would explain to her research team, "is about developing the capacity to create relational possibilities where others see only limitations."

Her mother Maria's wisdom echoed in these moments of profound romantic exploration. "True love," Maria would say, "is not about achieving a predetermined version of partnership. It's about creating space for mutual emotional evolution and individual liberation."

Rosa Martinez observed this transformation with profound appreciation. "You're not just analyzing romantic interactions," Rosa would tell her. "You're creating entire new ecosystems of emotional possibility."

Elena's work demonstrated that love as a source of strength was a sophisticated form of collective and individual imagination. Each romantic challenge became an opportunity for deeper understanding, for more nuanced personal and relational integration.

The boundaries between personal growth, emotional intelligence, and romantic connection became increasingly fluid. Elena Rodriguez was not just a researcher or a technologist. She was an architect of romantic possibility, continuously reimagining the very concept of human potential for deep, transformative emotional connection.

Her platforms were never just about technological solutions. They were always about human potential, about creating broader pathways of emotional understanding and creative reimagination.

As romantic landscapes continued to shift and transform, Elena Rodriguez stood at their complex intersection—not as an observer, but as a creative force of continuous emotional exploration.

Her approach was fundamentally revolutionary. Love as a source of strength was not about achieving a fixed state of romantic perfection. It was about creating comprehensive ecosystems of emotional potential, about developing broader pathways of continuous human and relational growth.

Emotional refinement, she was demonstrating, was never a destination. It was always a journey of endless, beautiful becoming—a continuous process of creating more expansive, more authentic ways of understanding human potential for deep, meaningful romantic connection.

In the intricate dance of emotional exploration, Elena Rodriguez had discovered something profound: that true emotional resilience was not about perfect relationship realization. It was about creating spaces of mutual understanding, about developing the capacity to grow, to learn, and to continuously reimagine the possibilities of human romantic potential.

Chapter 30: Professional Breakthrough

30.1 Achieving Career Milestones

Professional success for Elena Rodriguez was never a simple accumulation of achievements. It was a complex, multidimensional ecosystem of innovation, strategic thinking, and profound human potential—a sophisticated intersection of technological innovation, ethical considerations, and transformative professional vision.

Her approach to career milestones emerged from an intricate family legacy of professional resilience and intellectual ambition. Rodriguez ' professional tradition was not about climbing corporate ladders or accumulating accolades, but about creating meaningful, transformative systems that could reshape entire fields of human endeavor.

Carlos Rodriguez had been her first professional mentor. "Professional success," he would tell her during their strategic conversations that blended technological insight with philosophical depth, "is about creating ecosystems of possibility, not just individual achievements."

The technological platforms Elena developed were far more than professional tools. They were comprehensive frameworks of innovation—adaptive systems that could recognize complex professional challenges, identify transformative opportunities, and create personalized strategies for meaningful professional growth and collective understanding.

Her collaboration with international research teams and industry leaders provided a unique lens for understanding professional breakthrough. They didn't just analyze existing professional paradigms; they created collaborative ecosystems of innovation potential, challenging traditional notions of career development and technological advancement.

Rosa Martinez, her longtime mentor, recognized the extraordinary depth of Elena's professional exploration. "You're not just analyzing professional patterns," Rosa would observe during their profound discussions. "You're systematically deconstructing and reimagining entire landscapes of professional potential."

Each professional challenge became a site of profound research. Not in a clinical, detached sense, but as a genuine exploration of human capacity for transformative innovation. Elena understood that professional success was never about achieving a fixed state of accomplishment. It was about creating expansive spaces of continuous learning and professional transformation.

Her work challenged traditional professional paradigms. Career milestones were not simply a matter of individual achievement, but a sophisticated system that offered profound insights into human potential for collective professional innovation.

The international collaborations that explored professional innovation were more than academic or corporate pursuits. They were comprehensive explorations of technological potential, human capability, and the intricate dynamics of professional understanding and advancement.

Her approach was fundamentally revolutionary. Professional breakthrough was not about achieving predetermined career objectives, but about creating new frameworks of individual and collective professional potential and innovative liberation.

30.2 Overcoming Professional Barriers

Professional barriers were not immovable obstacles for Elena Rodriguez. They were sophisticated challenges to be systematically deconstructed, reimagined, and transformed—a complex strategy of professional navigation that extended far beyond traditional notions of career advancement.

Her technological and research background provided a unique lens for understanding the intricate landscapes of professional potential. She approached professional challenges with the same systematic curiosity she applied to complex technological and social systems. Each professional barrier became a dataset, each career challenge a system waiting to be understood and transcended.

Marcus, her research collaborator, was fascinated by her approach. "You're developing a comprehensive framework of professional evolution," he observed. "Not just overcoming barriers, but creating entire ecosystems of professional potential."

Elena developed what she called a "professional liberation framework"—a comprehensive approach to understanding and transforming career potential. The framework had multiple sophisticated components:

1. **Professional Topology**: Mapping complex career landscapes
2. **Barrier Translation Mechanisms**: Identifying and interpreting professional constraints
3. **Transformative Career Strategies**: Developing approaches to meaningful professional growth

Her conversations with Gabriel became profound explorations of professional potential. They didn't just discuss career challenges. They created comprehensive models of how human beings could transform professional barriers into sites of radical innovative breakthrough.

"Professional limitations," Gabriel would argue, "are often just poorly understood systems of human potential waiting to be reimagined."

The technological tools Elena developed were extraordinary. Adaptive professional assessment platforms that could recognize complex patterns of career interaction, that could create personalized strategies for navigating the most intricate professional landscapes.

But these were never just about technological solutions. They were always about human potential, about creating broader pathways of professional understanding and innovative liberation.

Her work began to attract international attention. Industry leaders, researchers, and innovation experts all recognized that she was developing something far more profound than traditional career development methodologies. She was creating a comprehensive approach to understanding human potential for transformative professional innovation.

The Rodriguez family's professional resilience provided a crucial contextual framework. Generations had navigated complex professional landscapes, understanding that true career advancement was about survival, collective understanding, and continuous professional adaptation.

International collaborations and research initiatives became sites of extraordinary professional exploration. Elena wasn't just studying professional dynamics; she was creating comprehensive dialogues about the future of professional potential and human empowerment.

30.3 The Culmination of Professional Ambition

Professional ambition, for Elena Rodriguez, was never a linear trajectory of achievement. It was a living, breathing ecosystem of innovative potential—a continuous process of reimagining professional existence that extended far beyond traditional notions of career success.

Her approach to professional potential challenged every conventional narrative of career development. Where traditional approaches saw professional ambition as a predetermined path, Elena saw it as complex, adaptive systems offering profound insights into human capacity for comprehensive professional transformation.

The technological platforms she developed merged sophisticated professional assessment algorithms with deep philosophical and sociological insights. These weren't just career development tools. They were comprehensive ecosystems of professional potential—platforms that could recognize complex professional patterns and create transformative strategies for meaningful career growth.

"Professional fulfillment," she would explain to her research team, "is about developing the capacity to create professional possibilities where others see only limitations."

Her mother Maria's wisdom echoed in these moments of profound professional exploration. "True professional ambition," Maria would say, "is not about achieving a predetermined version of success. It's about creating space for collective innovation and individual professional liberation."

Rosa Martinez observed this transformation with profound appreciation. "You're not just analyzing professional interactions," Rosa would tell her. "You're creating entire new ecosystems of professional possibility."

Elena's work demonstrated that the culmination of professional ambition was a sophisticated form of collective and individual imagination. Each professional challenge became an opportunity for deeper understanding, for more nuanced personal and collective professional integration.

The boundaries between personal growth, technological innovation, and professional understanding became increasingly fluid. Elena Rodriguez was not just a researcher or a technologist. She was an architect of professional possibility, continuously reimagining the very concept of human potential for transformative career innovation.

Her platforms were never just about technological solutions. They were always about human potential, about creating broader pathways of professional understanding and creative reimagination.

As professional landscapes continued to shift and transform, Elena Rodriguez stood at their complex intersection—not as an observer, but as a creative force of continuous professional exploration.

Her approach was fundamentally revolutionary. The culmination of professional ambition was not about achieving a fixed state of career perfection. It was about creating comprehensive ecosystems of professional potential, about developing broader pathways of continuous human and career growth.

Professional refinement, she was demonstrating, was never a destination. It was always a journey of endless, beautiful becoming—a continuous process of creating more expansive, more authentic ways of understanding human potential for transformative professional innovation.

In the intricate dance of professional exploration, Elena Rodriguez had discovered something profound: that true career fulfillment was not about perfect professional realization. It was about creating spaces of mutual understanding, about developing the capacity to grow, to learn, and to continuously reimagine the possibilities of human professional potential.

Chapter 31: Psychological Insight

31.1 Deepening Self-Understanding

Psychological awareness was never a passive journey of introspection for Elena Rodriguez. It was a dynamic, transformative process of continuously exploring the intricate landscapes of human consciousness—a sophisticated intersection of technological innovation, philosophical inquiry, and profound human potential.

Her approach to psychological understanding emerged from a rich family legacy of emotional intelligence and intellectual curiosity. The Rodriguez psychological tradition was not about surface-level self-analysis, but about creating living, breathing ecosystems of internal exploration—dynamic frameworks that could adapt, evolve, and transform the very essence of human self-perception.

Carlos Rodriguez, her father, had been her first mentor of psychological exploration. "Self-understanding," he would tell her during their profound conversations that blended scientific precision with philosophical depth, "is not about discovering a fixed identity. It's about creating a continuous process of internal discovery and reimagination."

The technological platforms Elena developed were far more than psychological assessment tools. They were comprehensive psychological exploration systems—adaptive frameworks that could recognize complex internal patterns, identify emergent aspects of consciousness, and create personalized strategies for deep psychological growth and collective understanding.

Her collaboration with international psychological researchers provided a unique lens for understanding the depths of human consciousness. They didn't just analyze existing psychological frameworks; they created collaborative ecosystems of psychological potential, challenging traditional notions of mental functioning and human awareness.

Rosa Martinez, her longtime mentor, recognized the extraordinary depth of Elena's psychological exploration. "You're not just analyzing psychological patterns," Rosa would observe during their intimate discussions. "You're systematically deconstructing and reimagining entire landscapes of human consciousness."

Each psychological challenge became a site of profound research. Not in a clinical, detached sense, but as a genuine exploration of human capacity for internal transformation. Elena understood that psychological awareness was never about achieving a fixed state of self-understanding. It was about creating expansive spaces of continuous learning and psychological evolution.

Her work challenged traditional psychological paradigms. Self-understanding was not simply a matter of introspective analysis, but a sophisticated information system that offered profound insights into human potential for collective psychological growth.

The international research collaborations that explored psychological innovation were more than academic pursuits. They were comprehensive explorations of consciousness boundaries, technological potential, and the intricate dynamics of human psychological understanding.

Her approach was fundamentally revolutionary. Psychological awareness was not about achieving internal certainty, but about creating new frameworks of collective psychological potential and individual mental liberation.

31.2 Navigating Internal Landscapes

Internal navigation was not a linear journey for Elena Rodriguez. It was a sophisticated strategy of understanding the complex terrains of human consciousness, of creating more expansive, more authentic frameworks of emotional and psychological dynamics.

Her technological and psychological background provided a unique lens for understanding the intricate landscapes of internal potential. She approached psychological challenges with the same systematic curiosity she applied to complex technological and cognitive systems. Each internal encounter became a dataset, each emotional experience a system waiting to be understood and expanded.

Marcus, her research collaborator, was fascinated by her approach. "You're developing a comprehensive framework of psychological evolution," he observed. "Not just navigating internal challenges, but creating entire ecosystems of psychological potential."

Elena developed what she called an "internal navigation framework"—a comprehensive approach to understanding and transforming psychological potential. The framework had multiple sophisticated components:

1. **Consciousness Topology**: Mapping complex internal landscapes
2. **Emotional Translation Mechanisms**: Identifying and interpreting psychological patterns
3. **Transformative Psychological Strategies**: Developing approaches to meaningful internal growth

Her conversations with Gabriel became profound explorations of psychological potential. They didn't just discuss emotional challenges. They created comprehensive models of how human beings could transform internal barriers into sites of radical psychological innovation.

"Psychological limitations," Gabriel would argue, "are often just poorly understood systems of human emotional capability waiting to be reimagined."

The technological tools Elena developed were extraordinary. Adaptive psychological assessment platforms that could recognize complex patterns of internal interaction, that could create personalized strategies for navigating the most intricate emotional landscapes.

But these were never just about technological solutions. They were always about human potential, about creating broader pathways of psychological understanding and emotional liberation.

Her work began to attract international attention. Psychologists, neuroscientists, and emotional intelligence experts all recognized that she was developing something far more profound than traditional psychological methodologies. She was creating a comprehensive approach to understanding human potential for deep, transformative internal exploration.

The Rodriguez family's psychological resilience provided a crucial contextual framework. Generations had navigated complex internal landscapes, understanding that true emotional intelligence was about survival, collective understanding, and continuous psychological adaptation.

International collaborations and research initiatives became sites of extraordinary psychological exploration. Elena wasn't just studying psychological dynamics; she was creating comprehensive dialogues about the future of psychological potential and human emotional empowerment.

31.3 The Power of Self-Reflection

Self-reflection, for Elena Rodriguez, was never a passive act of internal observation. It was a living, breathing ecosystem of psychological potential—a continuous process of reimagining internal existence that extended far beyond traditional notions of psychological development.

Her approach to psychological potential challenged every conventional narrative of mental growth. Where traditional approaches saw self-reflection as a static practice, Elena saw it as complex, adaptive systems offering profound insights into human capacity for comprehensive psychological transformation.

The technological platforms she developed merged sophisticated psychological assessment algorithms with deep philosophical and sociological insights. These weren't just introspection tools. They were comprehensive ecosystems of psychological potential—platforms that could recognize complex internal patterns and create transformative strategies for meaningful psychological growth.

"Self-reflection," she would explain to her research team, "is about developing the capacity to create internal possibilities where others see only limitations."

Her mother Maria's wisdom echoed in these moments of profound psychological exploration. "True psychological growth," Maria would say, "is not about achieving a predetermined version of self. It's about creating space for individual psychological evolution and internal liberation."

Rosa Martinez observed this transformation with profound appreciation. "You're not just analyzing internal interactions," Rosa would tell her. "You're creating entire new ecosystems of psychological possibility."

Elena's work demonstrated that the power of self-reflection was a sophisticated form of collective and individual imagination. Each psychological challenge became an opportunity for deeper understanding, for more nuanced personal and collective internal integration.

The boundaries between personal growth, technological innovation, and psychological understanding became increasingly fluid. Elena Rodriguez was not just a researcher or a technologist. She was an architect of psychological possibility, continuously reimagining the very concept of human potential for transformative internal exploration.

Her platforms were never just about technological solutions. They were always about human potential, about creating broader pathways of psychological understanding and creative reimagination.

As psychological landscapes continued to shift and transform, Elena Rodriguez stood at their complex intersection—not as an observer, but as a creative force of continuous psychological exploration.

Her approach was fundamentally revolutionary. The power of self-reflection was not about achieving a fixed state of psychological perfection. It was about creating comprehensive ecosystems of psychological potential, about developing broader pathways of continuous human and internal growth.

Psychological refinement, she was demonstrating, was never a destination. It was always a journey of endless, beautiful becoming—a continuous process of creating more expansive, more authentic ways of understanding human potential for transformative internal exploration.

In the intricate dance of psychological reflection, Elena Rodriguez had discovered something profound: that true psychological growth was not about perfect self-realization. It was about creating spaces of mutual understanding, about developing the capacity to grow, to learn, and to continuously reimagine the possibilities of human psychological potential.

Chapter 32: Social Revolution

32.1 Challenging Social Norms

Social transformation was never a passive process for Elena Rodriguez. It was a dynamic, multidimensional ecosystem of collective reimagination—a sophisticated intersection of technological innovation, sociological insight, and profound human potential for radical social change.

Her approach to challenging social norms emerged from a deep familial legacy of social resilience and collective understanding. The Rodriguez tradition was not about incremental adjustments to existing social structures, but about creating entirely new frameworks of collective human potential that could fundamentally reshape social landscapes.

Carlos Rodriguez had been her first mentor of social innovation. "Social change," he would explain during their intricate conversations that wove together technological precision and philosophical depth, "is about creating ecosystems of possibility that challenge the very foundations of collective understanding."

The technological platforms Elena developed were far more than social analysis tools. They were comprehensive frameworks of social transformation—adaptive systems that could recognize complex social patterns, identify transformative opportunities, and create personalized strategies for meaningful collective growth and social reimagination.

Her collaboration with international social researchers and change innovators provided a unique lens for understanding social revolution. They didn't just analyze existing social structures; they created collaborative ecosystems of social potential, challenging traditional notions of collective organization and human interaction.

Rosa Martinez, her longtime mentor, recognized the extraordinary depth of Elena's social exploration. "You're not just analyzing social patterns," Rosa would observe during their profound discussions. "You're systematically deconstructing and reimagining entire landscapes of collective human potential."

Each social challenge became a site of profound research. Not in a clinical, detached sense, but as a genuine exploration of human capacity for collective transformation. Elena understood that challenging social norms was never about achieving a fixed state of social perfection. It was about creating expansive spaces of continuous learning and social evolution.

Her work challenged traditional sociological paradigms. Social transformation was not simply a matter of institutional change, but a sophisticated system that offered profound insights into human potential for collective social innovation.

The international collaborations that explored social innovation were more than academic pursuits. They were comprehensive explorations of human potential, technological innovation, and the intricate dynamics of social understanding and collective reimagination.

Her approach was fundamentally revolutionary. Social revolution was not about achieving predetermined social objectives, but about creating new frameworks of collective potential and social liberation.

32.2 Redefining Social Boundaries

Social boundaries were not immovable constraints for Elena Rodriguez. They were sophisticated challenges to be systematically deconstructed, reimagined, and transformed—a complex strategy of social navigation that extended far beyond traditional notions of collective limitation.

Her technological and research background provided a unique lens for understanding the intricate landscapes of social potential. She approached social challenges with the same systematic curiosity she applied to complex technological and human systems. Each social boundary became a dataset, each collective constraint a system waiting to be understood and transcended.

Marcus, her research collaborator, was fascinated by her approach. "You're developing a comprehensive framework of social evolution," he observed. "Not just challenging boundaries, but creating entire ecosystems of collective potential."

Elena developed what she called a "social liberation framework"—a comprehensive approach to understanding and transforming collective potential. The framework had multiple sophisticated components:

1. **Social Topology**: Mapping complex collective landscapes
2. **Boundary Translation Mechanisms**: Identifying and interpreting social constraints
3. **Transformative Social Strategies**: Developing approaches to meaningful collective growth

Her conversations with Gabriel became profound explorations of social potential. They didn't just discuss social challenges. They created comprehensive models of how human beings could transform social barriers into sites of radical collective innovation.

"Social limitations," Gabriel would argue, "are often just poorly understood systems of human potential waiting to be reimagined."

The technological tools Elena developed were extraordinary. Adaptive social assessment platforms that could recognize complex patterns of collective interaction, that could create personalized strategies for navigating the most intricate social landscapes.

But these were never just about technological solutions. They were always about human potential, about creating broader pathways of collective understanding and social liberation.

Her work began to attract international attention. Social innovators, researchers, and change experts all recognized that she was developing something far more profound than traditional social change methodologies. She was creating a comprehensive approach to understanding human potential for transformative social innovation.

The Rodriguez family's social resilience provided a crucial contextual framework. Generations had navigated complex social landscapes, understanding that true social transformation was about survival, collective understanding, and continuous social adaptation.

International collaborations and research initiatives became sites of extraordinary social exploration. Elena wasn't just studying social dynamics; she was creating comprehensive dialogues about the future of social potential and human collective empowerment.

32.3 The Evolution of Social Perception

Social perception, for Elena Rodriguez, was never a static construct. It was a living, breathing ecosystem of collective potential—a continuous process of reimagining social existence that extended far beyond traditional notions of societal understanding.

Her approach to social potential challenged every conventional narrative of collective development. Where traditional approaches saw social perception as a fixed set of collective beliefs, Elena saw it as complex, adaptive systems offering profound insights into human capacity for comprehensive social transformation.

The technological platforms she developed merged sophisticated social analysis algorithms with deep philosophical and anthropological insights. These weren't just social research tools. They were comprehensive ecosystems of collective potential—platforms that could recognize complex social patterns and create transformative strategies for meaningful social growth.

"Social change," she would explain to her research team, "is about developing the capacity to create collective possibilities where others see only limitations."

Her mother Maria's wisdom echoed in these moments of profound social exploration. "True social evolution," Maria would say, "is not about achieving a predetermined version of collective existence. It's about creating space for collective innovation and social liberation."

Rosa Martinez observed this transformation with profound appreciation. "You're not just analyzing social interactions," Rosa would tell her. "You're creating entire new ecosystems of collective possibility."

Elena's work demonstrated that the evolution of social perception was a sophisticated form of collective imagination. Each social challenge became an opportunity for deeper understanding, for more nuanced collective and individual social integration.

The boundaries between personal growth, technological innovation, and social understanding became increasingly fluid. Elena Rodriguez was not just a researcher or a technologist. She was an architect of social possibility, continuously reimagining the very concept of human potential for transformative collective innovation.

Her platforms were never just about technological solutions. They were always about human potential, about creating broader pathways of social understanding and creative reimagination.

As social landscapes continued to shift and transform, Elena Rodriguez stood at their complex intersection—not as an observer, but as a creative force of continuous social exploration.

Her approach was fundamentally revolutionary. The evolution of social perception was not about achieving a fixed state of collective perfection. It was about creating comprehensive ecosystems of social potential, about developing broader pathways of continuous human and collective growth.

Social refinement, she was demonstrating, was never a destination. It was always a journey of endless, beautiful becoming—a continuous process of creating more expansive, more authentic ways of understanding human potential for transformative social innovation.

In the intricate dance of social exploration, Elena Rodriguez had discovered something profound: that true social change was not about perfect collective realization. It was about creating spaces of mutual understanding, about developing the capacity to grow, to learn, and to continuously reimagine the possibilities of human collective potential.

Chapter 33: Emotional Mastery

33.1 Developing Emotional Control

Emotional regulation was never a simple mechanism of suppression for Elena Rodriguez. It was a complex, dynamic ecosystem of psychological sophistication—a profound intersection of technological innovation, psychological insight, and human potential for transformative emotional understanding.

Her approach to emotional control emerged from a rich family legacy of psychological resilience and emotional intelligence. The Rodriguez emotional tradition was not about constraining feelings, but about creating adaptive frameworks that could navigate the most intricate emotional landscapes with precision, compassion, and strategic insight.

Carlos Rodriguez had been her first mentor of emotional strategy. "Emotional control," he would explain during their nuanced conversations that blended scientific precision with philosophical depth, "is about developing a comprehensive understanding of internal emotional dynamics—not about limitation, but about expansive potential."

The technological platforms Elena developed were far more than emotional assessment tools. They were comprehensive frameworks of emotional regulation—adaptive systems that could recognize complex emotional patterns, identify transformative opportunities, and create personalized strategies for meaningful emotional growth and collective understanding.

Her collaboration with international psychological researchers provided a unique lens for understanding the depths of emotional control. They didn't just analyze existing emotional frameworks; they created collaborative ecosystems of emotional potential, challenging traditional notions of psychological functioning and human feeling.

Rosa Martinez, her longtime mentor, recognized the extraordinary depth of Elena's emotional exploration. "You're not just analyzing emotional patterns," Rosa would observe during their intimate discussions. "You're systematically deconstructing and reimagining entire landscapes of human emotional potential."

Each emotional challenge became a site of profound research. Not in a clinical, detached sense, but as a genuine exploration of human capacity for internal transformation. Elena understood that emotional control was never about achieving a fixed state of emotional suppression. It was about creating expansive spaces of continuous learning and emotional evolution.

Her work challenged traditional psychological paradigms. Emotional regulation was not simply a matter of controlling feelings, but a sophisticated information system that offered profound insights into human potential for collective emotional growth.

The international research collaborations that explored emotional innovation were more than academic pursuits. They were comprehensive explorations of emotional boundaries, technological potential, and the intricate dynamics of human emotional understanding.

Her approach was fundamentally revolutionary. Emotional control was not about achieving internal certainty, but about creating new frameworks of collective emotional potential and individual emotional liberation.

33.2 Navigating Emotional Complexity

Emotional navigation was not a linear journey for Elena Rodriguez. It was a sophisticated strategy of understanding the complex terrains of human feelings, of creating more expansive, more authentic frameworks of emotional dynamics.

Her technological and psychological background provided a unique lens for understanding the intricate landscapes of emotional potential. She approached emotional challenges with the same systematic curiosity she applied to complex technological and cognitive systems. Each emotional encounter became a dataset, each feeling experience a system waiting to be understood and expanded.

Marcus, her research collaborator, was fascinated by her approach. "You're developing a comprehensive framework of emotional evolution," he observed. "Not just navigating emotional challenges, but creating entire ecosystems of emotional potential."

Elena developed what she called an "emotional navigation framework"—a comprehensive approach to understanding and transforming emotional potential. The framework had multiple sophisticated components:

1. **Emotional Topology**: Mapping complex internal emotional landscapes
2. **Feeling Translation Mechanisms**: Identifying and interpreting emotional patterns
3. **Transformative Emotional Strategies**: Developing approaches to meaningful internal emotional growth

Her conversations with Gabriel became profound explorations of emotional potential. They didn't just discuss emotional challenges. They created comprehensive models of how human beings could transform internal emotional barriers into sites of radical emotional innovation.

"Emotional limitations," Gabriel would argue, "are often just poorly understood systems of human emotional capability waiting to be reimagined."

The technological tools Elena developed were extraordinary. Adaptive emotional assessment platforms that could recognize complex patterns of internal emotional interaction, that could create personalized strategies for navigating the most intricate emotional landscapes.

But these were never just about technological solutions. They were always about human potential, about creating broader pathways of emotional understanding and emotional liberation.

Her work began to attract international attention. Psychologists, neuroscientists, and emotional intelligence experts all recognized that she was developing something far more profound than traditional emotional methodology. She was creating a comprehensive approach to understanding human potential for deep, transformative emotional exploration.

The Rodriguez family's emotional resilience provided a crucial contextual framework. Generations had navigated complex emotional landscapes, understanding that true emotional intelligence was about survival, collective understanding, and continuous emotional adaptation.

International collaborations and research initiatives became sites of extraordinary emotional exploration. Elena wasn't just studying emotional dynamics; she was creating comprehensive dialogues about the future of emotional potential and human emotional empowerment.

33.3 The Art of Emotional Balance

Emotional balance, for Elena Rodriguez, was never a passive state of equilibrium. It was a living, breathing ecosystem of emotional potential—a continuous process of reimagining internal emotional existence that extended far beyond traditional notions of psychological stability.

Her approach to emotional potential challenged every conventional narrative of emotional development. Where traditional approaches saw emotional balance as a static condition, Elena saw it as complex, adaptive systems offering profound insights into human capacity for comprehensive emotional transformation.

The technological platforms she developed merged sophisticated emotional assessment algorithms with deep philosophical and sociological insights. These weren't just emotional regulation tools. They were comprehensive ecosystems of emotional potential—platforms that could recognize complex emotional patterns and create transformative strategies for meaningful emotional growth.

"Emotional resilience," she would explain to her research team, "is about developing the capacity to create internal emotional possibilities where others see only limitations."

Her mother Maria's wisdom echoed in these moments of profound emotional exploration. "True emotional balance," Maria would say, "is not about achieving a predetermined version of emotional stability. It's about creating space for individual emotional evolution and internal liberation."

Rosa Martinez observed this transformation with profound appreciation. "You're not just analyzing internal emotional interactions," Rosa would tell her. "You're creating entire new ecosystems of emotional possibility."

Elena's work demonstrated that the art of emotional balance was a sophisticated form of collective and individual imagination. Each emotional challenge became an opportunity for deeper understanding, for more nuanced personal and collective emotional integration.

The boundaries between personal growth, technological innovation, and emotional understanding became increasingly fluid. Elena Rodriguez was not just a researcher or a technologist. She was an architect of emotional possibility, continuously reimagining the very concept of human potential for transformative emotional exploration.

Her platforms were never just about technological solutions. They were always about human potential, about creating broader pathways of emotional understanding and creative reimagination.

As emotional landscapes continued to shift and transform, Elena Rodriguez stood at their complex intersection—not as an observer, but as a creative force of continuous emotional exploration.

Her approach was fundamentally revolutionary. The art of emotional balance was not about achieving a fixed state of emotional perfection. It was about creating comprehensive ecosystems of emotional potential, about developing broader pathways of continuous human and internal emotional growth.

Emotional refinement, she was demonstrating, was never a destination. It was always a journey of endless, beautiful becoming—a continuous process of creating more expansive, more authentic ways of understanding human potential for transformative emotional exploration.

In the intricate dance of emotional resilience, Elena Rodriguez had discovered something profound: that true emotional balance was not about perfect emotional realization. It was about creating spaces of mutual understanding, about developing the capacity to grow, to learn, and to continuously reimagine the possibilities of human emotional potential.

Chapter 34: Romantic Wisdom

34.1 Understanding Romantic Dynamics

Romantic wisdom was never a simple accumulation of experiences for Elena Rodriguez. It was a profound philosophical ecosystem of human connection—a complex interplay of emotional intelligence, strategic understanding, and transformative potential that extended far beyond traditional notions of love and intimate relationships.

Her approach to romantic dynamics emerged from a rich tapestry of intellectual and emotional exploration. Love was not a passive state to be experienced, but an active terrain of continuous negotiation, growth, and mutual transformation. Each romantic encounter became a sophisticated landscape of potential—a nuanced dialogue between individual histories, emotional architectures, and collective human potential.

Carlos Rodriguez, her father, had been her first mentor of relational complexity. "Romantic wisdom," he would explain during their intricate conversations that blended psychological insight with philosophical depth, "is about developing a comprehensive understanding of human connection—not about achieving a predetermined state of romantic perfection, but about creating expansive frameworks of mutual understanding."

The technological and psychological platforms Elena developed were far more than relationship assessment tools. They were comprehensive frameworks of romantic intelligence—adaptive systems that could recognize complex relational patterns, identify transformative opportunities, and create personalized strategies for meaningful emotional and interpersonal growth.

Her international collaborations with sociologists, psychologists, and relationship researchers provided a unique lens for understanding the intricate dynamics of romantic connection. They didn't just analyze existing relationship frameworks; they created collaborative ecosystems of romantic potential, challenging traditional notions of love, intimacy, and human connection.

Rosa Martinez, her longtime mentor, recognized the extraordinary depth of Elena's romantic exploration. "You're not just analyzing relationship patterns," Rosa would observe during their intimate discussions. "You're systematically deconstructing and reimagining entire landscapes of human romantic potential."

Each romantic challenge became a site of profound research. Not in a clinical, detached sense, but as a genuine exploration of human capacity for deep, transformative connection. Elena understood that romantic wisdom was never about achieving a fixed state of relational stability. It was about creating expansive spaces of continuous learning and interpersonal evolution.

Her work challenged traditional romantic paradigms. Romantic understanding was not simply a matter of managing feelings or maintaining relationships. It was a sophisticated information system that offered profound insights into human potential for collective emotional and relational growth.

The international research collaborations that explored romantic innovation were more than academic pursuits. They were comprehensive explorations of emotional boundaries, technological potential, and the intricate dynamics of human intimate understanding.

Her approach was fundamentally revolutionary. Romantic wisdom was not about achieving internal or external certainty, but about creating new frameworks of collective romantic potential and individual emotional liberation.

34.2 Navigating Intimate Connections

Romantic navigation was not a linear journey for Elena Rodriguez. It was a sophisticated strategy of understanding the complex terrains of human intimate connections, of creating more expansive, more authentic frameworks of relational dynamics.

Her technological and psychological background provided a unique lens for understanding the intricate landscapes of romantic potential. She approached romantic challenges with the same systematic curiosity she applied to complex technological and cognitive systems. Each romantic encounter became a dataset, each relationship experience a system waiting to be understood and expanded.

Marcus, her research collaborator, was fascinated by her approach. "You're developing a comprehensive framework of romantic evolution," he observed. "Not just navigating romantic challenges, but creating entire ecosystems of relational potential."

Elena developed what she called a "romantic navigation framework"—a comprehensive approach to understanding and transforming romantic potential. The framework had multiple sophisticated components:

1. **Relational Topology**: Mapping complex intimate emotional landscapes
2. **Connection Translation Mechanisms**: Identifying and interpreting intricate relational patterns
3. **Transformative Romantic Strategies**: Developing approaches to meaningful interpersonal emotional growth

Her conversations with Gabriel became profound explorations of romantic potential. They didn't just discuss romantic challenges. They created comprehensive models of how human beings could transform internal relational barriers into sites of radical romantic innovation.

"Romantic limitations," Gabriel would argue, "are often just poorly understood systems of human relational capability waiting to be reimagined."

The technological tools Elena developed were extraordinary. Adaptive romantic assessment platforms that could recognize complex patterns of intimate emotional interaction, that could create personalized strategies for navigating the most intricate relational landscapes.

But these were never just about technological solutions. They were always about human potential, about creating broader pathways of romantic understanding and emotional liberation.

Her work began to attract international attention. Relationship experts, sociologists, and emotional intelligence researchers all recognized that she was developing something far more profound than traditional romantic methodology. She was creating a comprehensive approach to understanding human potential for deep, transformative romantic exploration.

The Rodriguez family's relational resilience provided a crucial contextual framework. --Generations had navigated complex romantic landscapes, understanding that true romantic wisdom was about survival, collective understanding, and continuous relational adaptation.

International collaborations and research initiatives became sites of extraordinary romantic exploration. Elena wasn't just studying romantic dynamics; she was creating comprehensive dialogues about the future of romantic potential and human emotional empowerment.

34.3 Love as a Source of Wisdom

Love, for Elena Rodriguez, was never a passive emotional state. It was a living, breathing ecosystem of transformative potential—a continuous process of reimagining intimate human existence that extended far beyond traditional narratives of romantic connection.

Her approach to romantic potential challenged every conventional narrative of love and relationships. Where traditional approaches saw love as a static condition, Elena saw it as complex, adaptive systems offering profound insights into human capacity for comprehensive emotional and relational transformation.

The technological platforms she developed merged sophisticated romantic assessment algorithms with deep philosophical and sociological insights. These weren't just relationship management tools. They were comprehensive ecosystems of romantic potential—platforms that could recognize complex relational patterns and create transformative strategies for meaningful emotional and interpersonal growth.

"Romantic wisdom," she would explain to her research team, "is about developing the capacity to create intimate emotional possibilities where others see only limitations."

Her mother Maria's wisdom echoed in these moments of profound romantic exploration. "True love," Maria would say, "is not about achieving a predetermined version of romantic stability. It's about creating space for individual and collective emotional evolution and intimate liberation."

Rosa Martinez observed this transformation with profound appreciation. "You're not just analyzing intimate emotional interactions," Rosa would tell her. "You're creating entire new ecosystems of romantic possibility."

Elena's work demonstrated that love as a source of wisdom was a sophisticated form of collective and individual imagination. Each romantic challenge became an opportunity for deeper understanding, for more nuanced personal and collective emotional integration.

The boundaries between personal growth, technological innovation, and romantic understanding became increasingly fluid. Elena Rodriguez was not just a researcher or a technologist. She was an architect of romantic possibility, continuously reimagining the very concept of human potential for transformative intimate exploration.

Her platforms were never just about technological solutions. They were always about human potential, about creating broader pathways of romantic understanding and creative reimagination.

As romantic landscapes continued to shift and transform, Elena Rodriguez stood at their complex intersection—not as an observer, but as a creative force of continuous romantic exploration.

Her approach was fundamentally revolutionary. Love as a source of wisdom was not about achieving a fixed state of romantic perfection. It was about creating comprehensive ecosystems of romantic potential, about developing broader pathways of continuous human and intimate emotional growth.

Romantic refinement, she was demonstrating, was never a destination. It was always a journey of endless, beautiful becoming—a continuous process of creating more expansive, more authentic ways of understanding human potential for transformative romantic exploration.

In the intricate dance of intimate connection, Elena Rodriguez had discovered something profound: that true romantic wisdom was not about perfect relational realization. It was about creating spaces of mutual understanding, about developing the capacity to grow, to learn, and to continuously reimagine the possibilities of human romantic potential.

Chapter 35: Economic Strategy

35.1 Developing Financial Acumen

Financial intelligence was never merely about numbers for Elena Rodriguez. It was a sophisticated ecosystem of economic understanding—a complex intersection of technological innovation, market psychology, and human potential for transformative financial growth.

Her approach to economic strategy emerged from a profound understanding of both technological systems and human behavior. The Rodriguez family history had taught her that true financial acumen went far beyond simple profit calculations. It was about creating adaptive frameworks that could navigate the most intricate economic landscapes with precision, insight, and strategic sophistication.

Marcus Chen, her economic mentor, had helped shape her unique perspective. "Financial intelligence," he would explain during their detailed analytical sessions that merged market theory with practical application, "is about developing a comprehensive understanding of economic dynamics—not about accumulation, but about creating sustainable frameworks for growth."

The technological platforms Elena developed transcended traditional financial analysis tools. They were comprehensive frameworks of economic intelligence—adaptive systems that could recognize complex market patterns, identify transformative opportunities, and create personalized strategies for meaningful financial growth and collective prosperity.

Her collaboration with international economists provided an extraordinary lens for understanding the depths of economic potential. They didn't just analyze existing market frameworks; they created collaborative ecosystems of financial innovation, challenging traditional notions of economic success and human potential.

Sofia Martinez, her economic research partner, recognized the revolutionary nature of Elena's financial exploration. "You're not just analyzing market patterns," Sofia would observe during their strategic sessions. "You're systematically deconstructing and reimagining entire landscapes of economic potential."

Each financial challenge became a site of profound research. Not in a purely theoretical sense, but as a genuine exploration of human capacity for economic transformation. Elena understood that financial acumen was never about achieving a fixed state of wealth. It was about creating expansive spaces of continuous learning and economic evolution.

Her work challenged traditional financial paradigms. Economic intelligence was not simply a matter of managing assets or maximizing returns. It was a sophisticated information system that offered profound insights into human potential for collective financial growth and social transformation.

The international research collaborations that explored economic innovation were more than academic pursuits. They were comprehensive explorations of market boundaries, technological potential, and the intricate dynamics of human financial understanding.

Her approach was fundamentally revolutionary. Financial acumen was not about achieving economic certainty, but about creating new frameworks of collective financial potential and individual economic liberation.

35.2 Strategic Financial Planning

Economic navigation was not a linear journey for Elena Rodriguez. It was a sophisticated strategy of understanding the complex terrains of financial systems, of creating more expansive, more authentic frameworks of economic dynamics.

Her technological and psychological background provided a unique lens for understanding the intricate landscapes of financial potential. She approached economic challenges with the same systematic curiosity she applied to complex technological and cognitive systems. Each market interaction became a dataset, each financial experience a system waiting to be understood and expanded.

Gabriel, her investment strategist, was captivated by her approach. "You're developing a comprehensive framework of economic evolution," he observed. "Not just navigating financial challenges, but creating entire ecosystems of economic potential."

Elena developed what she called an "economic navigation framework"—a comprehensive approach to understanding and transforming financial potential. The framework had multiple sophisticated components:

1. **Economic Topology**: Mapping complex financial landscapes
2. **Market Translation Mechanisms**: Identifying and interpreting economic patterns
3. **Transformative Financial Strategies**: Developing approaches to meaningful economic growth

Her conversations with Rosa became profound explorations of economic potential. They didn't just discuss financial challenges. They created comprehensive models of how individuals and organizations could transform economic barriers into sites of radical financial innovation.

"Economic limitations," Rosa would argue, "are often just poorly understood systems of human financial capability waiting to be reimagined."

The technological tools Elena developed were extraordinary. Adaptive financial assessment platforms that could recognize complex patterns of market interaction, that could create personalized strategies for navigating the most intricate economic landscapes.

But these were never just about technological solutions. They were always about human potential, about creating broader pathways of financial understanding and economic liberation.

Her work began to attract international attention. Financial experts, economists, and market researchers all recognized that she was developing something far more profound than traditional economic methodology. She was creating a comprehensive approach to understanding human potential for deep, transformative financial exploration.

The Rodriguez family's economic resilience provided a crucial contextual framework. Generations had navigated complex financial landscapes, understanding that true economic wisdom was about survival, collective understanding, and continuous market adaptation.

International collaborations and research initiatives became sites of extraordinary economic exploration. Elena wasn't just studying market dynamics; she was creating comprehensive dialogues about the future of financial potential and human economic empowerment.

35.3 Wealth as a Tool for Transformation

Economic empowerment, for Elena Rodriguez, was never simply about financial accumulation. It was a living, breathing ecosystem of transformative potential—a continuous process of reimagining financial existence that extended far beyond traditional notions of wealth creation.

Her approach to economic potential challenged every conventional narrative of financial success. Where traditional approaches saw wealth as a static condition, Elena saw it as complex, adaptive systems offering profound insights into human capacity for comprehensive economic transformation.

The technological platforms she developed merged sophisticated financial assessment algorithms with deep sociological and psychological insights. These weren't just wealth management tools. They were comprehensive ecosystems of economic potential—platforms that could recognize complex market patterns and create transformative strategies for meaningful financial growth.

"Economic empowerment," she would explain to her research team, "is about developing the capacity to create financial possibilities where others see only limitations."

Her father Carlos's wisdom echoed in these moments of profound economic exploration. "True wealth," Carlos would say, "is not about achieving a predetermined version of financial success. It's about creating space for individual and collective economic evolution and financial liberation."

Marcus observed this transformation with profound appreciation. "You're not just analyzing market interactions," Marcus would tell her. "You're creating entire new ecosystems of economic possibility."

Elena's work demonstrated that wealth as a tool for transformation was a sophisticated form of collective and individual imagination. Each financial challenge became an opportunity for deeper understanding, for more nuanced personal and collective economic integration.

The boundaries between personal growth, technological innovation, and economic understanding became increasingly fluid. Elena Rodriguez was not just a researcher or a technologist. She was an architect of financial possibility, continuously reimagining the very concept of human potential for transformative economic exploration.

Her platforms were never just about technological solutions. They were always about human potential, about creating broader pathways of economic understanding and creative reimagination.

As financial landscapes continued to shift and transform, Elena Rodriguez stood at their complex intersection—not as an observer, but as a creative force of continuous economic exploration.

Her approach was fundamentally revolutionary. Wealth as a tool for transformation was not about achieving a fixed state of financial perfection. It was about creating comprehensive ecosystems of economic potential, about developing broader pathways of continuous human and financial growth.

Economic refinement, she was demonstrating, was never a destination. It was always a journey of endless, beautiful becoming—a continuous process of creating more expansive, more authentic ways of understanding human potential for transformative financial exploration.

In the intricate dance of economic empowerment, Elena Rodriguez had discovered something profound: that true financial transformation was not about perfect wealth realization. It was about creating spaces of mutual understanding, about developing the capacity to grow, to learn, and to continuously reimagine the possibilities of human economic potential.

Chapter 36: Moral Complexity

36.1 Exploring Ethical Nuances

Moral sophistication was never a matter of simple right and wrong for Elena Rodriguez. It was an intricate ecosystem of ethical understanding—a complex intersection of technological responsibility, human psychology, and the transformative potential of ethical decision-making.

Her approach to moral complexity emerged from years of wrestling with the ethical implications of technological innovation. The Rodriguez family legacy had taught her that true ethical understanding went beyond binary choices. It was about creating adaptive frameworks that could navigate the most intricate moral landscapes with precision, compassion, and philosophical depth.

Dr. Sarah Chen, her ethics mentor at the institute, had helped shape her nuanced perspective. "Moral sophistication," she would explain during their profound discussions that merged ethical theory with practical application, "is about developing a comprehensive understanding of human choice—not about moral absolutism, but about creating sustainable frameworks for ethical growth."

The ethical frameworks Elena developed transcended traditional moral analysis. They were comprehensive systems of ethical intelligence—adaptive approaches that could recognize complex patterns of moral decision-making, identify transformative opportunities, and create personalized strategies for meaningful ethical growth and collective understanding.

Her collaboration with international ethicists provided an extraordinary lens for understanding the depths of moral complexity. They didn't just analyze existing ethical frameworks; they created collaborative ecosystems of moral innovation, challenging traditional notions of right and wrong in the age of technological advancement.

Marcus Martinez, her research partner in ethical AI, recognized the revolutionary nature of Elena's moral exploration. "You're not just analyzing ethical patterns," Marcus would observe during their strategic sessions. "You're systematically deconstructing and reimagining entire landscapes of moral potential."

Each ethical challenge became a site of profound research. Not in a purely theoretical sense, but as a genuine exploration of human capacity for moral transformation. Elena understood that ethical sophistication was never about achieving a fixed state of moral certainty. It was about creating expansive spaces of continuous learning and ethical evolution.

Her work challenged traditional moral paradigms. Ethical intelligence was not simply a matter of following rules or maximizing utility. It was a sophisticated information system that offered profound insights into human potential for collective moral growth and social transformation.

The international research collaborations that explored ethical innovation were more than academic pursuits. They were comprehensive explorations of moral boundaries, technological responsibility, and the intricate dynamics of human ethical understanding.

Her approach was fundamentally revolutionary. Moral sophistication was not about achieving ethical certainty, but about creating new frameworks of collective moral potential and individual ethical liberation.

36.2 Navigating Moral Dilemmas

Ethical navigation was not a linear journey for Elena Rodriguez. It was a sophisticated strategy of understanding the complex terrains of moral decision-making, of creating more expansive, more authentic frameworks of ethical dynamics.

Her technological and psychological background provided a unique lens for understanding the intricate landscapes of moral potential. She approached ethical challenges with the same systematic curiosity she applied to complex technological and cognitive systems. Each moral decision became a dataset, each ethical experience a system waiting to be understood and expanded.

Rosa, her longtime colleague in ethical research, was captivated by her approach. "You're developing a comprehensive framework of moral evolution," she observed. "Not just navigating ethical challenges, but creating entire ecosystems of moral potential."

Elena developed what she called an "ethical navigation framework"—a comprehensive approach to understanding and transforming moral potential. The framework had multiple sophisticated components:

1. **Moral Topology**: Mapping complex ethical landscapes
2. **Ethical Translation Mechanisms**: Identifying and interpreting moral patterns
3. **Transformative Ethical Strategies**: Developing approaches to meaningful moral growth

Her conversations with Gabriel became profound explorations of ethical potential. They didn't just discuss moral challenges. They created comprehensive models of how individuals and organizations could transform ethical barriers into sites of radical moral innovation.

"Ethical limitations," Gabriel would argue, "are often just poorly understood systems of human moral capability waiting to be reimagined."

The frameworks Elena developed were extraordinary. Adaptive ethical assessment approaches that could recognize complex patterns of moral interaction, that could create personalized strategies for navigating the most intricate ethical landscapes.

But these were never just about theoretical solutions. They were always about human potential, about creating broader pathways of ethical understanding and moral liberation.

Her work began to attract international attention. Ethics experts, philosophers, and moral researchers all recognized that she was developing something far more profound than traditional ethical methodology. She was creating a comprehensive approach to understanding human potential for deep, transformative moral exploration.

The Rodriguez family's ethical resilience provided a crucial contextual framework. Generations had navigated complex moral landscapes, understanding that true ethical wisdom was about survival, collective understanding, and continuous moral adaptation.

International collaborations and research initiatives became sites of extraordinary ethical exploration. Elena wasn't just studying moral dynamics;

she was creating comprehensive dialogues about the future of ethical potential and human moral empowerment.

36.3 The Refinement of Personal Ethics

Moral growth, for Elena Rodriguez, was never simply about following established ethical principles. It was a living, breathing ecosystem of transformative potential—a continuous process of reimagining ethical existence that extended far beyond traditional notions of moral development.

Her approach to ethical potential challenged every conventional narrative of moral progress. Where traditional approaches saw ethics as a static condition, Elena saw it as complex, adaptive systems offering profound insights into human capacity for comprehensive moral transformation.

The frameworks she developed merged sophisticated ethical assessment methodologies with deep sociological and psychological insights. These weren't just moral decision-making tools. They were comprehensive ecosystems of ethical potential—approaches that could recognize complex moral patterns and create transformative strategies for meaningful ethical growth.

"Moral growth," she would explain to her research team, "is about developing the capacity to create ethical possibilities where others see only limitations."

Her mother Maria's wisdom echoed in these moments of profound ethical exploration. "True moral refinement," Maria would say, "is not about achieving a predetermined version of ethical perfection. It's about creating space for individual and collective moral evolution and ethical liberation."

Sarah observed this transformation with profound appreciation. "You're not just analyzing moral interactions," Sarah would tell her. "You're creating entire new ecosystems of ethical possibility."

Elena's work demonstrated that the refinement of personal ethics was a sophisticated form of collective and individual imagination. Each moral challenge became an opportunity for deeper understanding, for more nuanced personal and collective ethical integration.

The boundaries between personal growth, technological innovation, and ethical understanding became increasingly fluid. Elena Rodriguez was not just a researcher or a technologist. She was an architect of moral possibility, continuously reimagining the very concept of human potential for transformative ethical exploration.

Her frameworks were never just about theoretical solutions. They were always about human potential, about creating broader pathways of ethical understanding and creative reimagination.

As moral landscapes continued to shift and transform, Elena Rodriguez stood at their complex intersection—not as an observer, but as a creative force of continuous ethical exploration.

Her approach was fundamentally revolutionary. The refinement of personal ethics was not about achieving a fixed state of moral perfection. It was about creating comprehensive ecosystems of ethical potential, about developing broader pathways of continuous human and moral growth.

Ethical refinement, she was demonstrating, was never a destination. It was always a journey of endless, beautiful becoming—a continuous process of creating more expansive, more authentic ways of understanding human potential for transformative moral exploration.

In the intricate dance of ethical development, Elena Rodriguez had discovered something profound: that true moral growth was not about perfect ethical realization. It was about creating spaces of mutual understanding, about developing the capacity to grow, to learn, and to continuously reimagine the possibilities of human moral potential.

Chapter 37: Intellectual Mastery

37.1 Developing Intellectual Depth

Intellectual sophistication was never merely about accumulating knowledge for Elena Rodriguez. It was an intricate ecosystem of cognitive understanding—a complex intersection of technological innovation, neural processing, and the transformative potential of human thought.

Her approach to intellectual mastery emerged from years of exploring the boundaries of human cognition. The Rodriguez family tradition had taught her that true mental sophistication went beyond simple information retention. It was about creating adaptive frameworks that could navigate the most intricate intellectual landscapes with precision, creativity, and philosophical depth.

Dr. James Chen, her cognitive science mentor, had helped shape her sophisticated perspective. "Mental sophistication," he would explain during their profound discussions that merged neuroscience with technological innovation, "is about developing a comprehensive understanding of human thought—not about intellectual superiority, but about creating sustainable frameworks for cognitive growth."

The cognitive frameworks Elena developed transcended traditional learning models. They were comprehensive systems of intellectual intelligence—adaptive approaches that could recognize complex patterns of thought, identify transformative opportunities, and create personalized strategies for meaningful cognitive growth and collective understanding.

Her collaboration with international cognitive scientists provided an extraordinary lens for understanding the depths of mental complexity. They didn't just analyze existing learning frameworks; they created collaborative ecosystems of intellectual innovation, challenging traditional notions of knowledge acquisition and cognitive development.

Rosa Martinez, her research partner in cognitive enhancement, recognized the revolutionary nature of Elena's intellectual exploration. "You're not just analyzing cognitive patterns," Rosa would observe during their research sessions. "You're systematically deconstructing and reimagining entire landscapes of mental potential."

Each intellectual challenge became a site of profound research. Not in a purely theoretical sense, but as a genuine exploration of human capacity for cognitive transformation. Elena understood that mental sophistication was never about achieving a fixed state of knowledge. It was about creating expansive spaces of continuous learning and intellectual evolution.

Her work challenged traditional cognitive paradigms. Intellectual intelligence was not simply a matter of processing information or solving problems. It was a sophisticated system that offered profound insights into human potential for collective mental growth and cognitive transformation.

The international research collaborations that explored cognitive innovation were more than academic pursuits. They were comprehensive explorations of mental boundaries, technological enhancement, and the intricate dynamics of human intellectual understanding.

Her approach was fundamentally revolutionary. Mental sophistication was not about achieving cognitive certainty, but about creating new frameworks of collective intellectual potential and individual cognitive liberation.

37.2 Challenging Intellectual Boundaries

Cognitive exploration was not a linear journey for Elena Rodriguez. It was a sophisticated strategy of understanding the complex terrains of human thought, of creating more expansive, more authentic frameworks of intellectual dynamics.

Her technological and psychological background provided a unique lens for understanding the intricate landscapes of cognitive potential. She approached intellectual challenges with the same systematic curiosity she applied to complex technological and neural systems. Each mental process became a dataset, each cognitive experience a system waiting to be understood and expanded.

Marcus, her colleague in cognitive research, was captivated by her approach. "You're developing a comprehensive framework of intellectual evolution," he observed. "Not just navigating cognitive challenges, but creating entire ecosystems of mental potential."

Elena developed what she called a "cognitive navigation framework"—a comprehensive approach to understanding and transforming intellectual potential. The framework had multiple sophisticated components:

1. **Mental Topology**: Mapping complex cognitive landscapes
2. **Thought Translation Mechanisms**: Identifying and interpreting intellectual patterns
3. **Transformative Cognitive Strategies**: Developing approaches to meaningful mental growth

Her conversations with Gabriel became profound explorations of intellectual potential. They didn't just discuss cognitive challenges. They created comprehensive models of how individuals could transform mental barriers into sites of radical cognitive innovation.

"Intellectual limitations," Gabriel would argue, "are often just poorly understood systems of human cognitive capability waiting to be reimagined."

The frameworks Elena developed were extraordinary. Adaptive cognitive assessment approaches that could recognize complex patterns of mental interaction, that could create personalized strategies for navigating the most intricate intellectual landscapes.

But these were never just about theoretical solutions. They were always about human potential, about creating broader pathways of cognitive understanding and intellectual liberation.

Her work began to attract international attention. Cognitive scientists, philosophers, and learning researchers all recognized that she was developing something far more profound than traditional educational methodology. She was creating a comprehensive approach to understanding human potential for deep, transformative intellectual exploration.

The Rodriguez family's cognitive resilience provided a crucial contextual framework. Generations had navigated complex intellectual landscapes, understanding that true mental wisdom was about survival, collective understanding, and continuous cognitive adaptation.

International collaborations and research initiatives became sites of extraordinary intellectual exploration. Elena wasn't just studying cognitive dynamics; she was creating comprehensive dialogues about the future of mental potential and human intellectual empowerment.

37.3 The Pursuit of Intellectual Excellence

Continuous learning, for Elena Rodriguez, was never simply about acquiring new information. It was a living, breathing ecosystem of transformative potential—a continuous process of reimagining cognitive existence that extended far beyond traditional notions of education and knowledge acquisition.

Her approach to intellectual potential challenged every conventional narrative of learning progress. Where traditional approaches saw education as a linear process, Elena saw it as complex, adaptive systems offering profound insights into human capacity for comprehensive cognitive transformation.

The frameworks she developed merged sophisticated learning assessment methodologies with deep neurological and psychological insights. These weren't just educational tools. They were comprehensive ecosystems of intellectual potential—approaches that could recognize complex cognitive patterns and create transformative strategies for meaningful mental growth.

"Continuous learning," she would explain to her research team, "is about developing the capacity to create cognitive possibilities where others see only limitations."

Her father Carlos's wisdom echoed in these moments of profound intellectual exploration. "True mental excellence," Carlos would say, "is not about achieving a predetermined version of cognitive perfection. It's about creating space for individual and collective intellectual evolution and cognitive liberation."

James observed this transformation with profound appreciation. "You're not just analyzing learning patterns," James would tell her. "You're creating entire new ecosystems of intellectual possibility."

Elena's work demonstrated that the pursuit of intellectual excellence was a sophisticated form of collective and individual imagination. Each cognitive challenge became an opportunity for deeper understanding, for more nuanced personal and collective mental integration.

The boundaries between personal growth, technological innovation, and cognitive understanding became increasingly fluid. Elena Rodriguez was not just a researcher or a technologist. She was an architect of intellectual possibility, continuously reimagining the very concept of human potential for transformative cognitive exploration.

Her frameworks were never just about theoretical solutions. They were always about human potential, about creating broader pathways of mental understanding and creative reimagination.

As cognitive landscapes continued to shift and transform, Elena Rodriguez stood at their complex intersection—not as an observer, but as a creative force of continuous intellectual exploration.

Her approach was fundamentally revolutionary. The pursuit of intellectual excellence was not about achieving a fixed state of mental perfection. It was about creating comprehensive ecosystems of cognitive potential, about developing broader pathways of continuous human and intellectual growth.

Mental refinement, she was demonstrating, was never a destination. It was always a journey of endless, beautiful becoming—a continuous process of creating more expansive, more authentic ways of understanding human potential for transformative cognitive exploration.

In the intricate dance of intellectual development, Elena Rodriguez had discovered something profound: that true mental growth was not about perfect cognitive realization. It was about creating spaces of mutual understanding, about developing the capacity to grow, to learn, and to continuously reimagine the possibilities of human intellectual potential.

Chapter 38: Personal Revolution

38.1 Radical Self-Transformation

Personal transformation was never a simple matter of self-improvement for Elena Rodriguez. It was an intricate ecosystem of human evolution—a complex intersection of technological innovation, psychological understanding, and the transformative potential of radical self-reinvention.

Her approach to personal revolution emerged from years of exploring the boundaries of human potential. The Rodriguez family legacy had taught her that true transformation went beyond superficial change. It was about creating adaptive frameworks that could navigate the most intricate landscapes of personal development with precision, authenticity, and philosophical depth.

Dr. Maya Chen, her transformation mentor, had helped shape her revolutionary perspective. "Personal reinvention," she would explain during their profound discussions that merged psychological theory with practical application, "is about developing a comprehensive understanding of human potential—not about external change, but about creating sustainable frameworks for authentic growth."

The transformative frameworks Elena developed transcended traditional self-help models. They were comprehensive systems of personal intelligence—adaptive approaches that could recognize complex patterns of human development, identify transformative opportunities, and create personalized strategies for meaningful growth and collective understanding.

Her collaboration with international psychologists provided an extraordinary lens for understanding the depths of personal revolution. They didn't just analyze existing transformation frameworks; they created collaborative ecosystems of human innovation, challenging traditional notions of self-development and personal evolution.

Rosa Martinez, her research partner in human potential, recognized the revolutionary nature of Elena's personal exploration. "You're not just analyzing transformation patterns," Rosa would observe during their sessions. "You're systematically deconstructing and reimagining entire landscapes of human potential."

Each personal challenge became a site of profound research. Not in a purely theoretical sense, but as a genuine exploration of human capacity for radical transformation. Elena understood that personal revolution was never about achieving a fixed state of being. It was about creating expansive spaces of continuous evolution and authentic becoming.

Her work challenged traditional development paradigms. Personal intelligence was not simply a matter of behavior modification or habit formation. It was a sophisticated system that offered profound insights into human potential for collective growth and individual transformation.

The international research collaborations that explored personal innovation were more than academic pursuits. They were comprehensive explorations of human boundaries, transformative potential, and the intricate dynamics of authentic self-actualization.

Her approach was fundamentally revolutionary. Personal reinvention was not about achieving a predetermined ideal, but about creating new frameworks of collective human potential and individual liberation.

38.2 Breaking Systemic Limitations

Personal liberation was not a linear journey for Elena Rodriguez. It was a sophisticated strategy of understanding the complex terrains of human limitation, of creating more expansive, more authentic frameworks of personal freedom.

Her technological and psychological background provided a unique lens for understanding the intricate landscapes of human potential. She approached personal limitations with the same systematic curiosity she applied to complex technological and psychological systems. Each barrier became a dataset, each constraint a system waiting to be understood and transcended.

Marcus, her colleague in transformation research, was captivated by her approach. "You're developing a comprehensive framework of human liberation," he observed. "Not just overcoming limitations, but creating entire ecosystems of personal potential."

Elena developed what she called a "liberation framework"—a comprehensive approach to understanding and transforming human limitations. The framework had multiple sophisticated components:

1. **Personal Topology**: Mapping complex landscapes of limitation
2. **Liberation Translation Mechanisms**: Identifying and interpreting patterns of constraint
3. **Transformative Freedom Strategies**: Developing approaches to meaningful personal liberation

Her conversations with Gabriel became profound explorations of human potential. They didn't just discuss personal limitations. They created comprehensive models of how individuals could transform systemic barriers into sites of radical personal innovation.

"Human limitations," Gabriel would argue, "are often just poorly understood systems of personal capability waiting to be reimagined."

The frameworks Elena developed were extraordinary. Adaptive assessment approaches that could recognize complex patterns of limitation, that could create personalized strategies for navigating the most intricate landscapes of personal constraint.

But these were never just about theoretical solutions. They were always about human potential, about creating broader pathways of personal understanding and authentic liberation.

Her work began to attract international attention. Psychologists, sociologists, and human potential researchers all recognized that she was developing something far more profound than traditional development methodology. She was creating a comprehensive approach to understanding human potential for deep, transformative personal liberation.

The Rodriguez family's revolutionary resilience provided a crucial contextual framework. Generations had navigated complex landscapes of limitation, understanding that true personal freedom was about survival, collective understanding, and continuous adaptation.

International collaborations and research initiatives became sites of extraordinary personal exploration. Elena wasn't just studying human limitations; she was creating comprehensive dialogues about the future of personal potential and human empowerment.

38.3 The Journey of Self-Actualization

Self-actualization, for Elena Rodriguez, was never simply about reaching predetermined potential. It was a living, breathing ecosystem of transformative possibility—a continuous process of reimagining human existence that extended far beyond traditional notions of personal development.

Her approach to personal empowerment challenged every conventional narrative of self-actualization. Where traditional approaches saw development as a linear process, Elena saw it as complex, adaptive systems offering profound insights into human capacity for comprehensive transformation.

The frameworks she developed merged sophisticated personal assessment methodologies with deep psychological and sociological insights. These weren't just development tools. They were comprehensive ecosystems of human potential—approaches that could recognize complex patterns of growth and create transformative strategies for meaningful personal evolution.

"Self-actualization," she would explain to her research team, "is about developing the capacity to create personal possibilities where others see only limitations."

Her mother Maria's wisdom echoed in these moments of profound personal exploration. "True empowerment," Maria would say, "is not about achieving a predetermined version of success. It's about creating space for individual and collective evolution and authentic liberation."

Maya observed this transformation with profound appreciation. "You're not just analyzing development patterns," Maya would tell her. "You're creating entire new ecosystems of human possibility."

Elena's work demonstrated that the journey of self-actualization was a sophisticated form of collective and individual imagination. Each personal challenge became an opportunity for deeper understanding, for more nuanced authentic integration.

The boundaries between personal growth, technological innovation, and human understanding became increasingly fluid. Elena Rodriguez was not just a researcher or a technologist. She was an architect of human possibility, continuously reimagining the very concept of personal potential for transformative exploration.

Her frameworks were never just about theoretical solutions. They were always about human potential, about creating broader pathways of personal understanding and creative reimagination.

As landscapes of human potential continued to shift and transform, Elena Rodriguez stood at their complex intersection—not as an observer, but as a creative force of continuous personal exploration.

Her approach was fundamentally revolutionary. The journey of self-actualization was not about achieving a fixed state of personal perfection. It was about creating comprehensive ecosystems of human potential, about developing broader pathways of continuous personal growth and authentic becoming.

Personal revolution, she was demonstrating, was never a destination. It was always a journey of endless, beautiful becoming—a continuous process of creating more expansive, more authentic ways of understanding human potential for transformative exploration.

In the intricate dance of personal development, Elena Rodriguez had discovered something profound: that true self-actualization was not about perfect realization. It was about creating spaces of authentic understanding, about developing the capacity to grow, to learn, and to continuously reimagine the possibilities of human potential.

Chapter 39: Romantic Transcendence

39.1 Elevating Romantic Perspectives

Romantic transcendence was never merely about relationship improvement for Elena Rodriguez. It was an intricate ecosystem of human connection—a complex intersection of emotional intelligence, psychological understanding, and the transformative potential of profound intimate bonds.

Her approach to relationship evolution emerged from years of exploring the boundaries of human connection. The Rodriguez family wisdom had taught her that true romantic transcendence went beyond conventional relationship dynamics. It was about creating adaptive frameworks that could navigate the most intricate landscapes of intimate connection with authenticity, depth, and philosophical sophistication.

Dr. Isabella Chen, her relationship dynamics mentor, had helped shape her transcendent perspective. "Romantic evolution," she would explain during their profound discussions that merged psychological insight with emotional wisdom, "is about developing a comprehensive understanding of human connection—not about perfecting relationships, but about creating sustainable frameworks for authentic intimacy."

The relationship frameworks Elena developed transcended traditional romantic models. They were comprehensive systems of emotional intelligence—adaptive approaches that could recognize complex patterns of human connection, identify transformative opportunities, and create personalized strategies for meaningful relationship growth and collective understanding.

Her collaboration with international relationship psychologists provided an extraordinary lens for understanding the depths of romantic transcendence. They didn't just analyze existing relationship frameworks; they created collaborative ecosystems of emotional innovation, challenging traditional notions of love and intimate connection.

Rosa Martinez, her research partner in relationship dynamics, recognized the revolutionary nature of Elena's romantic exploration. "You're not just analyzing relationship patterns," Rosa would observe during their sessions.

"You're systematically deconstructing and reimagining entire landscapes of human connection."

Each relationship challenge became a site of profound research. Not in a purely theoretical sense, but as a genuine exploration of human capacity for transcendent connection. Elena understood that romantic evolution was never about achieving a fixed state of relationship perfection. It was about creating expansive spaces of continuous growth and authentic intimacy.

Her work challenged traditional relationship paradigms. Emotional intelligence was not simply a matter of communication skills or conflict resolution. It was a sophisticated system that offered profound insights into human potential for collective growth and intimate transformation.

The international research collaborations that explored relationship innovation were more than academic pursuits. They were comprehensive explorations of emotional boundaries, transformative potential, and the intricate dynamics of authentic human connection.

Her approach was fundamentally revolutionary. Romantic evolution was not about achieving predetermined ideals, but about creating new frameworks of collective emotional potential and individual intimate liberation.

39.2 Navigating Profound Emotional Connections

The exploration of romantic depth was not a linear journey for Elena Rodriguez. It was a sophisticated strategy of understanding the complex terrains of human intimacy, of creating more expansive, more authentic frameworks of emotional connection.

Her technological and psychological background provided a unique lens for understanding the intricate landscapes of relationship potential. She approached emotional depth with the same systematic curiosity she applied to complex psychological and interpersonal systems. Each intimate dynamic became a dataset, each emotional pattern a system waiting to be understood and elevated.

Marcus, her colleague in relationship research, was captivated by her approach. "You're developing a comprehensive framework of intimate connection," he observed. "Not just deepening relationships, but creating entire ecosystems of emotional potential."

Elena developed what she called a "depth framework"—a comprehensive approach to understanding and transforming intimate connections. The framework had multiple sophisticated components:

1. **Emotional Topology**: Mapping complex landscapes of intimacy
2. **Connection Translation Mechanisms**: Identifying and interpreting patterns of deep bonding
3. **Transformative Relationship Strategies**: Developing approaches to meaningful emotional depth

Her conversations with Gabriel became profound explorations of intimate potential. They didn't just discuss relationship challenges. They created comprehensive models of how individuals could transform surface-level connections into sites of radical emotional innovation.

"Relationship limitations," Gabriel would argue, "are often just poorly understood systems of intimate capability waiting to be reimagined."

The frameworks Elena developed were extraordinary. Adaptive assessment approaches that could recognize complex patterns of emotional connection, that could create personalized strategies for navigating the most intricate landscapes of intimate relationship.

But these were never just about theoretical solutions. They were always about human potential, about creating broader pathways of emotional understanding and authentic connection.

Her work began to attract international attention. Relationship experts, psychologists, and human connection researchers all recognized that she was developing something far more profound than traditional relationship methodology. She was creating a comprehensive approach to understanding human potential for deep, transformative intimate connection.

The Rodriguez family's emotional wisdom provided a crucial contextual framework. Generations had navigated complex landscapes of intimacy, understanding that true romantic depth was about authenticity, collective understanding, and continuous growth.

International collaborations and research initiatives became sites of extraordinary relationship exploration. Elena wasn't just studying emotional patterns; she was creating comprehensive dialogues about the future of intimate potential and human connection.

39.3 Love as a Transformative Force

Emotional transcendence, for Elena Rodriguez, was never simply about deepening feelings. It was a living, breathing ecosystem of transformative possibility—a continuous process of reimagining human connection that extended far beyond traditional notions of love and relationship.

Her approach to romantic transformation challenged every conventional narrative of love. Where traditional approaches saw relationships as linear progressions, Elena saw them as complex, adaptive systems offering profound insights into human capacity for comprehensive emotional evolution.

The frameworks she developed merged sophisticated relationship assessment methodologies with deep psychological and spiritual insights. These weren't just relationship tools. They were comprehensive ecosystems of intimate potential—approaches that could recognize complex patterns of connection and create transformative strategies for meaningful emotional evolution.

"Love as transformation," she would explain to her research team, "is about developing the capacity to create relationship possibilities where others see only limitations."

Her mother Maria's wisdom echoed in these moments of profound relationship exploration. "True love," Maria would say, "is not about achieving a predetermined version of connection. It's about creating space for individual and collective evolution and authentic intimacy."

Isabella observed this transformation with profound appreciation. "You're not just analyzing relationship patterns," Isabella would tell her. "You're creating entire new ecosystems of intimate possibility."

Elena's work demonstrated that love as a transformative force was a sophisticated form of collective and individual imagination. Each relationship challenge became an opportunity for deeper understanding, for more nuanced authentic connection.

The boundaries between personal growth, emotional intelligence, and relationship understanding became increasingly fluid. Elena Rodriguez was not just a researcher or a relationship expert. She was an architect of intimate possibility, continuously reimagining the very concept of human potential for transformative connection.

Her frameworks were never just about theoretical solutions. They were always about human potential, about creating broader pathways of emotional understanding and creative reimagination.

As landscapes of human connection continued to shift and transform, Elena Rodriguez stood at their complex intersection—not as an observer, but as a creative force of continuous romantic exploration.

Her approach was fundamentally revolutionary. Love as a transformative force was not about achieving a fixed state of relationship perfection. It was about creating comprehensive ecosystems of emotional potential, about developing broader pathways of continuous intimate growth and authentic becoming.

Romantic transcendence, she was demonstrating, was never a destination. It was always a journey of endless, beautiful becoming—a continuous process of creating more expansive, more authentic ways of understanding human potential for transformative connection.

In the intricate dance of intimate evolution, Elena Rodriguez had discovered something profound: that true love was not about perfect relationship realization. It was about creating spaces of authentic understanding, about developing the capacity to grow, to connect, and to continuously reimagine the possibilities of human intimacy.

Chapter 40: Professional Mastery

40.1 Achieving Professional Excellence

For Elena Rodriguez, the pursuit of professional excellence had evolved far beyond conventional metrics of success. Having revolutionized the understanding of human relationships through her groundbreaking research, she now stood at the intersection of academic brilliance and practical innovation, where theoretical frameworks transformed into tangible solutions for human connection.

The international recognition of her work had created ripples across multiple disciplines. Universities worldwide were incorporating her relationship frameworks into their psychology curricula, while corporate entities sought her expertise in developing more humane, emotionally intelligent organizational cultures. Yet for Elena, this was merely the foundation of what she envisioned as true professional mastery.

Dr. Marcus Chen, her longtime colleague and friend, observed the unique nature of her approach. "What sets Elena apart," he noted during a keynote address at the International Psychology Conference, "is her ability to merge rigorous academic methodology with profound emotional intelligence. She's not just studying human connection—she's fundamentally reimagining how we understand professional excellence in the field of relationship psychology."

Her innovative methodologies had transcended traditional academic boundaries. The Rodriguez Framework, as it had come to be known, was being applied in diverse fields—from corporate leadership development to international conflict resolution. Each application revealed new dimensions of its potential, demonstrating the universal relevance of her insights into human connection.

The prestigious Princeton Center for Advanced Studies had created a dedicated research division focused solely on expanding and applying her methodologies. "Elena's work," the center's director Dr. Sarah Thompson explained, "represents a paradigm shift in how we approach professional excellence in psychological research. She's shown us that true mastery lies in creating frameworks that can evolve and adapt while maintaining their fundamental integrity."

Her collaboration with international research institutions had expanded into a global network of excellence. Teams across continents were building upon her foundational work, creating specialized applications for different cultural contexts while maintaining the core principles of authentic human connection that defined her approach.

The professional recognition, while gratifying, was secondary to Elena's primary mission. She understood that true professional mastery wasn't about accolades or institutional validation. It was about creating lasting impact, about developing frameworks that could continue to evolve and adapt long after their initial conception.

40.2 Overcoming Ultimate Professional Challenges

The path to professional mastery presented Elena with challenges that tested not just her expertise, but her fundamental understanding of what it meant to triumph in her field. The conventional metrics of success—peer recognition, institutional validation, publication impact—seemed increasingly inadequate as measures of true professional achievement.

Her work with the International Institute for Psychological Innovation had revealed the complexity of translating theoretical frameworks into practical applications across diverse cultural contexts. Each new implementation of her methodologies presented unique challenges that required not just adaptation, but fundamental reimagining of how relationship frameworks could serve different communities.

Dr. Isabella Martinez, her research partner in the institute's global initiatives, recognized the revolutionary nature of Elena's approach to professional challenges. "What others see as obstacles," Isabella observed, "Elena sees as opportunities for framework evolution. She's not just solving problems—she's creating entirely new paradigms of professional excellence."

The challenge of scaling her methodologies while maintaining their integrity had led to the development of what she called "adaptive excellence frameworks"—sophisticated systems that could maintain their core principles while evolving to meet specific contextual needs. These frameworks represented a breakthrough in how professional methodologies could be both universal and contextually specific.

Her work with international organizations had revealed the need for what she termed "professional transcendence"—moving beyond traditional notions of career success to create frameworks that could address the deepest challenges of human connection in an increasingly complex world.

The Harvard Review of Psychology dedicated an entire issue to examining the implications of her approach. "Rodriguez's work," the editorial stated, "represents not just professional excellence, but a fundamental reimagining of what excellence means in psychological research and practice."

Her collaboration with global research teams had evolved into what she called "collaborative mastery networks"—interconnected groups of professionals working to expand and adapt her methodologies while maintaining their essential integrity. These networks became living laboratories of professional excellence, constantly testing and refining approaches to human connection.

40.3 The Synthesis of Professional Ambition

The culmination of Elena's professional journey represented more than personal achievement—it was a synthesis of ambition and purpose that transcended traditional notions of career fulfillment. Her work had evolved into what she called a "holistic professional ecosystem," where individual success was inseparable from collective advancement.

The Rodriguez Institute for Human Connection, established in partnership with leading international universities, became a center for what she termed "transformative professional excellence"—a place where ambitious professionals could learn to merge rigorous methodology with profound emotional intelligence.

Dr. James Wilson, dean of the Psychology Department at Stanford, recognized the revolutionary nature of her approach to professional fulfillment. "Elena has shown us," he noted, "that true career satisfaction lies not in individual achievement, but in creating frameworks that enable collective growth and transformation."

Her work with global organizations had led to the development of what she called "fulfillment matrices"—sophisticated systems for understanding how professional excellence could align with personal purpose and collective benefit. These matrices became powerful tools for organizations seeking to create more meaningful, emotionally intelligent professional environments.

The international response to her frameworks had created what she termed "resonance networks"—interconnected communities of professionals working to expand and adapt her methodologies while maintaining their essential principles. These networks became living examples of how professional ambition could serve both individual and collective growth.

Her approach to professional fulfillment challenged conventional wisdom. Success wasn't measured by traditional metrics but by the capacity to create lasting positive impact. The Rodriguez Methodology, as it came to be known in professional circles, offered a new paradigm for understanding career satisfaction.

The synthesis of her professional journey had revealed something profound: true mastery wasn't about achieving predetermined goals but about creating frameworks that could continue to evolve and serve long after their initial conception. Her work had shown that professional excellence was inseparable from human connection and collective growth.

As Elena reflected on her professional journey, she understood that true mastery wasn't a destination but a continuous process of growth and adaptation. The frameworks she had developed would continue to evolve, serving as foundations for future innovations in understanding human connection and professional excellence.

In the end, her greatest professional triumph wasn't in the accolades or recognition, but in creating something that could continue to grow and serve beyond her direct involvement. She had shown that true professional mastery lay in developing frameworks that could adapt and evolve while maintaining their essential purpose: serving the deepest needs of human connection and understanding.

The synthesis of her professional ambition had revealed something fundamental: that true career fulfillment came not from achieving predetermined goals, but from creating lasting frameworks that could continue to serve and evolve. In this realization, Elena Rodriguez had not just achieved professional mastery—she had redefined what mastery meant in the context of human understanding and connection.

Chapter 41: Psychological Liberation

41.1 Breaking Psychological Constraints

The journey toward psychological liberation marked a profound evolution in Elena Rodriguez's understanding of human potential. Having achieved professional mastery and revolutionized the field of relationship psychology, she now turned her attention to what she considered the ultimate frontier: the liberation of the human mind from its self-imposed constraints.

Her groundbreaking work at the Rodriguez Institute had revealed patterns that transcended individual psychological limitations. These weren't merely personal barriers; they were systematic constraints that shaped how humans perceived their own potential for growth and transformation. Through years of research and practical application, Elena had begun to understand that true psychological freedom required more than traditional therapeutic approaches—it demanded a fundamental reimagining of human cognitive potential.

Dr. Sarah Chen, her research partner in cognitive psychology, recognized the revolutionary nature of Elena's approach. "What Elena has discovered," Sarah noted during their collaborative sessions, "isn't just another psychological framework. It's a complete paradigm shift in how we understand human potential for mental liberation."

The liberation methodologies Elena developed challenged conventional psychological wisdom. Rather than focusing on symptom management or behavioral modification, her approach centered on what she termed "cognitive transcendence"—the ability to recognize and move beyond inherited mental constraints that limited human potential for growth and transformation.

Her collaboration with international neuroscience teams had revealed surprising patterns in how psychological constraints formed and perpetuated themselves. These weren't just individual patterns but collective frameworks that shaped human perception and potential across cultures and contexts.

Isabella Martinez, her longtime colleague in psychological research, observed the transformative impact of Elena's work. "You're not just helping people overcome limitations," Isabella remarked. "You're showing them how to reimagine the very nature of psychological possibility."

The frameworks Elena developed for psychological liberation were extraordinary in their scope and sophistication. They combined cutting-edge neuroscience with deep psychological insight, creating practical methodologies for transcending mental constraints while maintaining psychological stability and growth.

41.2 Navigating Internal Transformation

The process of psychological rebirth, as Elena conceived it, was far more profound than traditional notions of personal transformation. It was about fundamentally reimagining the relationship between consciousness and potential, between inherited limitations and unlimited possibility.

Her work at the International Center for Psychological Innovation had revealed patterns in how humans navigated internal transformation. These weren't just individual journeys but collective processes that reflected deeper truths about human potential for psychological evolution and growth.

Dr. Marcus Thompson, leading the center's research division, recognized the revolutionary implications of Elena's approach. "What we're seeing here," he observed, "is nothing less than a complete reimagining of how humans can transform their psychological reality."

The transformation protocols Elena developed were sophisticated systems that could adapt to individual needs while maintaining their core principles of psychological liberation. These weren't just therapeutic tools but comprehensive frameworks for understanding and facilitating profound internal change.

Her collaboration with global consciousness researchers had expanded understanding of how psychological rebirth occurred across different cultural contexts. The patterns they discovered suggested universal principles underlying human potential for transformation and growth.

Rosa Hernandez, her partner in transformation research, noted the unique nature of Elena's approach. "You've created something extraordinary," Rosa observed. "Not just methods for change, but entire ecosystems of psychological possibility."

The frameworks for navigating internal transformation became living laboratories of human potential. Each application revealed new dimensions of possibility, new ways of understanding how humans could transcend psychological limitations and achieve genuine rebirth.

41.3 The Power of Self-Actualization

The culmination of Elena's work in psychological liberation revealed profound truths about human potential for self-actualization. This wasn't merely about achieving predetermined goals; it was about fundamentally reimagining what was possible in human psychological development.

Her research at the Rodriguez Institute had evolved into what she called "actualization ecosystems"—comprehensive frameworks that supported continuous psychological growth and transformation. These systems recognized that true empowerment came not from achieving fixed states but from developing the capacity for ongoing evolution and adaptation.

Dr. James Wilson, collaborating on international psychology initiatives, recognized the revolutionary nature of Elena's approach to self-actualization. "What Elena has created," he noted, "is nothing less than a new paradigm for understanding human potential for psychological empowerment."

The empowerment methodologies she developed were sophisticated systems that could recognize and support individual paths to self-actualization while maintaining connection to collective growth and transformation. These weren't just personal development tools but comprehensive frameworks for understanding human potential for psychological evolution.

Her work with global research teams had revealed patterns in how humans achieved genuine psychological empowerment. These patterns suggested universal principles underlying human capacity for self-actualization while acknowledging the unique nature of individual journeys.

Isabella Chen, observing the impact of Elena's work, noted its transformative potential. "You're not just helping people achieve goals," she remarked. "You're showing them how to reimagine their entire relationship with psychological possibility."

The frameworks Elena developed for psychological empowerment became living examples of what was possible in human development. Each application revealed new dimensions of potential, new ways of understanding how humans could achieve genuine self-actualization while maintaining authentic connection to others.

Her approach to psychological liberation had revealed something profound: that true empowerment wasn't about achieving predetermined states but about developing the capacity for continuous growth and transformation. The Rodriguez Methodology, as it came to be known in psychological circles, offered a new paradigm for understanding human potential for self-actualization.

As Elena reflected on the journey of psychological liberation, she understood that this wasn't merely about individual freedom or personal achievement. It was about creating frameworks that could support continuous human evolution while maintaining authentic connection to collective growth and transformation.

The power of self-actualization, she had discovered, lay not in reaching fixed goals but in developing the capacity for ongoing psychological evolution. Her work had shown that true empowerment came from creating spaces where individuals could continuously reimagine and reconstruct their relationship with psychological possibility.

In the end, Elena Rodriguez had done more than develop new psychological methodologies. She had created living frameworks for understanding and supporting human potential for continuous growth and transformation. Her work suggested that psychological liberation wasn't a destination but a continuous journey of discovery and evolution—a journey that could transform not just individuals but entire communities and cultures.

The synthesis of her work in psychological liberation had revealed something fundamental: that true freedom came not from escaping constraints but from developing the capacity to continuously reimagine and reconstruct psychological reality. In this understanding, Elena had not just achieved professional mastery—she had opened new pathways for human psychological evolution and growth.

Chapter 42: Social Metamorphosis

42.1 Radical Social Reimagining

The culmination of Elena Rodriguez's work in psychological liberation had naturally evolved into something even more profound: a fundamental reimagining of social structures and human collective potential. Having revolutionized understanding of individual psychological freedom, she now faced the ultimate challenge of translating these insights into broader social transformation.

The Rodriguez Institute had become more than a center for psychological research—it had evolved into a living laboratory for social metamorphosis. Elena understood that true social transformation required more than surface-level changes or policy adjustments. It demanded a complete reconceptualization of how humans could organize and relate to one another in more authentic, emotionally intelligent ways.

Dr. Maya Patel, her colleague in social systems research, recognized the revolutionary implications of Elena's approach. "What you're developing here," Maya observed during their strategic sessions, "isn't just another social theory. It's a complete paradigm shift in how we understand human collective potential."

The transformation frameworks Elena developed challenged conventional sociological wisdom. Rather than focusing on traditional metrics of social change, her methodologies centered on what she termed "collective consciousness evolution"—the capacity for entire communities to recognize and transcend inherited social constraints that limited human connection and collective growth.

Her collaboration with international social scientists had revealed surprising patterns in how social structures both enabled and constrained human potential. These weren't just institutional patterns but deeply embedded frameworks that shaped how humans imagined and created their collective reality.

Marcus Chen, leading the institute's social innovation division, noted the unprecedented nature of Elena's work. "You're not just studying social change," he remarked. "You're creating entirely new possibilities for human collective organization and authentic connection."

The methodologies Elena developed for social transformation were extraordinary in their sophistication and scope. They combined cutting-edge social science with deep psychological insight, creating practical frameworks for reimagining social structures while maintaining stability and promoting genuine human flourishing.

42.2 Challenging Fundamental Social Structures

Elena's approach to social rebellion transcended conventional notions of resistance or reform. Her work revealed that true social transformation required more than opposing existing structures—it demanded the creation of entirely new frameworks for human collective organization and connection.

The International Center for Social Innovation had become a hub for what Elena termed "constructive social rebellion"—approaches that didn't just challenge existing structures but actively created new possibilities for human collective organization. These weren't just theoretical models but living experiments in how humans could relate and organize differently.

Dr. Sarah Thompson, overseeing global social research initiatives, recognized the revolutionary potential of Elena's approach. "What we're witnessing," she noted, "is nothing less than a complete reimagining of how humans can structure their collective existence."

The rebellion frameworks Elena developed were sophisticated systems that could adapt to different cultural contexts while maintaining their core principles of social transformation. These weren't just protest methodologies but comprehensive approaches to creating new social possibilities.

Her work with global change agents had expanded understanding of how social transformation could occur across different cultural contexts. The patterns they discovered suggested universal principles underlying human potential for collective evolution while respecting cultural uniqueness.

Isabella Martinez, collaborating on international social initiatives, observed the unique nature of Elena's approach. "You've created something extraordinary," Isabella remarked. "Not just methods for change, but entire ecosystems of social possibility."

42.3 The Evolution of Social Consciousness

The culmination of Elena's work in social metamorphosis revealed profound truths about human collective potential. This wasn't merely about changing existing structures; it was about fundamentally reimagining what was possible in human social organization and collective consciousness.

Her research at the Rodriguez Institute had evolved into what she called "social consciousness ecosystems"—comprehensive frameworks that supported continuous collective evolution while maintaining authentic human connection. These systems recognized that true social transformation came not from achieving fixed states but from developing the capacity for ongoing collective adaptation and growth.

Dr. James Wilson, leading international social psychology initiatives, recognized the revolutionary nature of Elena's approach to social consciousness evolution. "What Elena has developed," he noted, "is nothing less than a new paradigm for understanding human collective potential."

The transformation methodologies she developed were sophisticated systems that could recognize and support unique cultural paths to social evolution while maintaining connection to universal principles of human growth and authentic connection. These weren't just social change tools but comprehensive frameworks for understanding human collective potential.

Her work with global research teams had revealed patterns in how human communities achieved genuine social transformation. These patterns suggested universal principles underlying human capacity for collective evolution while acknowledging the unique nature of different cultural contexts.

Rosa Hernandez, observing the impact of Elena's work in various communities, noted its transformative potential. "You're not just helping societies change," she remarked. "You're showing them how to reimagine their entire relationship with collective possibility."

The frameworks Elena developed for social consciousness evolution became living examples of what was possible in human collective development. Each application revealed new dimensions of potential, new ways of understanding how humans could achieve genuine social transformation while maintaining authentic connection to individual growth and cultural identity.

Her approach to social metamorphosis had revealed something profound: that true transformation wasn't about achieving predetermined social states but about developing the capacity for continuous collective evolution. The Rodriguez Methodology, as it came to be known in social science circles, offered a new paradigm for understanding human potential for collective transformation.

As Elena reflected on the journey of social metamorphosis, she understood that this wasn't merely about changing institutions or policies. It was about creating frameworks that could support continuous human collective evolution while maintaining authentic connection to psychological liberation and individual growth.

The evolution of social consciousness, she had discovered, lay not in reaching fixed social goals but in developing the capacity for ongoing collective transformation. Her work had shown that true social change came from creating spaces where communities could continuously reimagine and reconstruct their relationship with collective possibility.

In the end, Elena Rodriguez had done more than develop new social methodologies. She had created living frameworks for understanding and supporting human collective potential for continuous growth and transformation. Her work suggested that social metamorphosis wasn't a destination but a continuous journey of discovery and evolution—a journey that could transform not just communities but entire cultures and civilizations.

The synthesis of her work in social metamorphosis had revealed something fundamental: that true social transformation came not from opposing existing structures but from developing the capacity to continuously reimagine and reconstruct collective reality. In this understanding, Elena had not just achieved social innovation—she had opened new pathways for human collective evolution and authentic connection.

Chapter 43: Emotional Awakening

43.1 Profound Emotional Exploration

The natural progression of Elena Rodriguez's work in social metamorphosis had led her to an unexpected frontier: the depths of human emotional capacity. Having revolutionized understanding of social structures and collective consciousness, she now found herself drawn to explore the profound emotional landscapes that underpinned all human experience and transformation.

The Rodriguez Institute's Emotional Intelligence Division had evolved into something far more significant than its original scope—it had become a pioneering center for what Elena termed "emotional archaeology," delving into the deepest layers of human emotional capacity and understanding. She recognized that true emotional exploration required more than surface-level analysis or traditional psychological frameworks. It demanded a complete reconceptualization of how humans could access, understand, and integrate their deepest emotional experiences.

Dr. Alexandra Chen, leading the institute's emotional research initiatives, recognized the groundbreaking nature of Elena's approach. "What you're uncovering here," Alexandra observed during their research sessions, "isn't just another theory of emotional intelligence. It's a fundamental reimagining of human emotional potential."

The emotional exploration frameworks Elena developed challenged conventional psychological wisdom. Rather than focusing on traditional metrics of emotional intelligence, her methodologies centered on what she called "emotional consciousness evolution"—the capacity for individuals and communities to access and integrate deeper levels of emotional experience that had previously remained hidden or unexplored.

Her collaboration with international emotion researchers had revealed surprising patterns in how emotional depth both enabled and transformed human experience. These weren't just psychological patterns but deeply embedded frameworks that shaped how humans accessed and integrated their emotional reality.

David Kumar, heading the institute's emotional integration division, noted the unprecedented nature of Elena's discoveries. "You're not just studying emotional patterns," he remarked. "You're uncovering entirely new dimensions of human emotional capacity and authentic experience."

The methodologies Elena developed for emotional exploration were extraordinary in their sophistication and depth. They combined cutting-edge neuroscience with profound psychological insight, creating practical frameworks for accessing and integrating deeper emotional experiences while maintaining psychological stability and promoting genuine human flourishing.

43.2 Navigating Emotional Complexity

Elena's approach to emotional complexity transcended conventional notions of emotional intelligence or regulation. Her work revealed that true emotional navigation required more than managing emotions—it demanded the ability to embrace and integrate increasingly complex emotional states while maintaining authentic presence and connection.

The International Center for Emotional Research had become a hub for what Elena termed "constructive emotional complexity"—approaches that didn't just manage emotional states but actively created new possibilities for emotional experience and integration. These weren't just theoretical models but living experiments in how humans could access and navigate deeper emotional territories.

Dr. Rachel Thompson, overseeing global emotional research initiatives, recognized the transformative potential of Elena's approach. "What we're witnessing," she noted, "is nothing less than a complete reimagining of human emotional capacity and potential."

The navigation frameworks Elena developed were sophisticated systems that could adapt to different psychological contexts while maintaining their core principles of emotional exploration. These weren't just management techniques but comprehensive approaches to creating new possibilities for emotional experience and integration.

Her work with global emotion researchers had expanded understanding of how emotional complexity could be navigated across different cultural and psychological contexts. The patterns they discovered suggested universal principles underlying human potential for emotional evolution while respecting individual uniqueness.

Maria Santos, collaborating on international emotional initiatives, observed the unique nature of Elena's approach. "You've created something extraordinary," Maria remarked. "Not just methods for emotional management, but entire ecosystems of emotional possibility."

43.3 The Transformative Power of Emotion

The culmination of Elena's work in emotional awakening revealed profound truths about human emotional potential. This wasn't merely about understanding or managing emotions; it was about fundamentally reimagining what was possible in human emotional experience and development.

Her research at the Rodriguez Institute had evolved into what she called "emotional transformation ecosystems"—comprehensive frameworks that supported continuous emotional evolution while maintaining authentic human connection. These systems recognized that true emotional growth came not from achieving fixed states but from developing the capacity for ongoing emotional adaptation and integration.

Dr. Michael Chen, leading international emotional psychology initiatives, recognized the revolutionary nature of Elena's approach to emotional transformation. "What Elena has developed," he noted, "is nothing less than a new paradigm for understanding human emotional potential."

The transformation methodologies she developed were sophisticated systems that could recognize and support unique individual paths to emotional evolution while maintaining connection to universal principles of human growth and authentic experience. These weren't just emotional development tools but comprehensive frameworks for understanding human emotional potential.

Her work with global research teams had revealed patterns in how individuals achieved genuine emotional transformation. These patterns suggested universal principles underlying human capacity for emotional evolution while acknowledging the unique nature of individual psychological contexts.

Sophia Patel, observing the impact of Elena's work across various communities, noted its transformative potential. "You're not just helping people understand their emotions," she remarked. "You're showing them how to reimagine their entire relationship with emotional possibility."

The frameworks Elena developed for emotional transformation became living examples of what was possible in human emotional development. Each application revealed new dimensions of potential, new ways of understanding how humans could achieve genuine emotional transformation while maintaining authentic connection to individual growth and cultural identity.

Her approach to emotional awakening had revealed something profound: that true transformation wasn't about achieving predetermined emotional states but about developing the capacity for continuous emotional evolution. The Rodriguez Emotional Integration Methodology, as it came to be known in psychological circles, offered a new paradigm for understanding human potential for emotional transformation.

As Elena reflected on the journey of emotional awakening, she understood that this wasn't merely about managing or understanding emotions. It was about creating frameworks that could support continuous human emotional evolution while maintaining authentic connection to psychological liberation and individual growth.

The power of emotional transformation, she had discovered, lay not in reaching fixed emotional goals but in developing the capacity for ongoing emotional evolution. Her work had shown that true emotional growth came from creating spaces where individuals could continuously reimagine and reconstruct their relationship with emotional possibility.

In the end, Elena Rodriguez had done more than develop new emotional methodologies. She had created living frameworks for understanding and supporting human emotional potential for continuous growth and transformation. Her work suggested that emotional awakening wasn't a destination but a continuous journey of discovery and evolution—a journey that could transform not just individuals but entire communities and cultures.

The synthesis of her work in emotional awakening had revealed something fundamental: that true emotional transformation came not from controlling or managing emotions but from developing the capacity to continuously reimagine and reconstruct emotional reality. In this understanding, Elena had not just achieved emotional innovation—she had opened new pathways for human emotional evolution and authentic connection.

Chapter 44: Romantic Revelation

44.1 Uncovering Romantic Truths

Elena Rodriguez's groundbreaking work in emotional awakening had naturally led her to explore its most profound manifestation: the realm of romantic connection. Having revolutionized understanding of emotional capacity and transformation, she now found herself drawn to investigate the deepest truths underlying human romantic experience and potential.

The Relationship Studies Division at the Rodriguez Institute had evolved beyond conventional research parameters—it had become a pioneering center for what Elena termed "romantic consciousness exploration," delving into the fundamental nature of human intimate connection. She recognized that understanding authentic romantic truth required more than traditional relationship psychology or attachment theory. It demanded a complete reconceptualization of how humans could experience and understand profound intimate connection.

Dr. Sarah Williams, heading the institute's relationship research initiatives, recognized the revolutionary implications of Elena's approach. "What you're discovering here," Sarah observed during their analysis sessions, "isn't just another theory of romantic attachment. It's a fundamental reimagining of human capacity for intimate connection."

The romantic insight frameworks Elena developed challenged established relationship psychology. Rather than focusing on traditional metrics of relationship success, her methodologies centered on what she called "romantic consciousness evolution"—the capacity for individuals to access and integrate deeper levels of intimate connection that transcended conventional understanding of romantic relationships.

Her collaboration with international relationship researchers had revealed surprising patterns in how romantic connection both enabled and transformed human consciousness. These weren't just psychological patterns but deeply embedded frameworks that shaped how humans experienced and integrated their capacity for intimate connection.

Thomas Chen, leading the institute's relationship integration division, noted the unprecedented nature of Elena's discoveries. "You're not just studying relationship patterns," he remarked. "You're uncovering entirely new dimensions of human capacity for authentic intimate connection."

The methodologies Elena developed for understanding romantic truth were extraordinary in their sophistication and depth. They combined cutting-edge relationship science with profound psychological insight, creating practical frameworks for accessing and integrating deeper levels of romantic connection while maintaining individual authenticity and promoting genuine human flourishing.

44.2 Navigating Profound Intimate Connections

Elena's approach to intimate connection transcended conventional notions of relationship dynamics or romantic attachment. Her work revealed that true romantic depth required more than emotional intimacy—it demanded the ability to access and integrate increasingly profound levels of connection while maintaining authentic individual development.

The International Center for Relationship Research had become a hub for what Elena termed "constructive romantic depth"—approaches that didn't just examine relationship patterns but actively created new possibilities for profound intimate connection. These weren't just theoretical models but living experiments in how humans could access and navigate deeper territories of romantic experience.

Dr. Maya Patel, overseeing global relationship research initiatives, recognized the transformative potential of Elena's approach. "What we're witnessing," she noted, "is nothing less than a complete reimagining of human capacity for profound intimate connection."

The navigation frameworks Elena developed were sophisticated systems that could adapt to different relationship contexts while maintaining their core principles of romantic exploration. These weren't just relationship tools but comprehensive approaches to creating new possibilities for profound intimate connection and integration.

Her work with global relationship researchers had expanded understanding of how romantic depth could be accessed and navigated across different cultural and psychological contexts. The patterns they discovered suggested universal principles underlying human potential for romantic evolution while respecting individual and cultural uniqueness.

Isabella Martinez, collaborating on international relationship initiatives, observed the unique nature of Elena's approach. "You've created something extraordinary," Isabella remarked. "Not just methods for relationship development, but entire ecosystems of romantic possibility."

44.3 Love as a Source of Enlightenment

The culmination of Elena's work in romantic revelation had unveiled profound truths about human potential for intimate connection. This wasn't merely about understanding or improving relationships; it was about fundamentally reimagining what was possible in human romantic experience and consciousness development.

Her research at the Rodriguez Institute had evolved into what she called "romantic wisdom ecosystems"—comprehensive frameworks that supported continuous evolution of intimate connection while maintaining authentic individual growth. These systems recognized that true romantic wisdom came not from achieving fixed relationship states but from developing the capacity for ongoing romantic evolution and integration.

Dr. James Wilson, leading international relationship psychology initiatives, recognized the revolutionary nature of Elena's approach to romantic wisdom. "What Elena has developed," he noted, "is nothing less than a new paradigm for understanding human potential for profound intimate connection."

The transformation methodologies she developed were sophisticated systems that could recognize and support unique individual paths to romantic wisdom while maintaining connection to universal principles of human growth and authentic experience. These weren't just relationship development tools but comprehensive frameworks for understanding human potential for profound intimate connection.

Her work with global research teams had revealed patterns in how individuals achieved genuine romantic wisdom. These patterns suggested universal principles underlying human capacity for romantic evolution while acknowledging the unique nature of individual relationship contexts.

Laura Zhang, observing the impact of Elena's work across various communities, noted its transformative potential. "You're not just helping people understand relationships," she remarked. "You're showing them how to reimagine their entire relationship with romantic possibility."

The frameworks Elena developed for romantic wisdom became living examples of what was possible in human relationship development. Each application revealed new dimensions of potential, new ways of understanding how humans could achieve genuine romantic enlightenment while maintaining authentic connection to individual growth and cultural identity.

Her approach to romantic revelation had revealed something profound: that true relationship wisdom wasn't about achieving predetermined romantic states but about developing the capacity for continuous romantic evolution. The Rodriguez Relationship Wisdom Methodology, as it came to be known in psychological circles, offered a new paradigm for understanding human potential for romantic transformation.

As Elena reflected on the journey of romantic revelation, she understood that this wasn't merely about improving relationships or understanding attachment. It was about creating frameworks that could support continuous human romantic evolution while maintaining authentic connection to psychological liberation and individual growth.

The source of romantic wisdom, she had discovered, lay not in reaching fixed relationship goals but in developing the capacity for ongoing romantic evolution. Her work had shown that true relationship enlightenment came from creating spaces where individuals could continuously reimagine and reconstruct their relationship with romantic possibility.

In the end, Elena Rodriguez had done more than develop new relationship methodologies. She had created living frameworks for understanding and supporting human potential for continuous growth and transformation through intimate connection. Her work suggested that romantic revelation wasn't a destination but a continuous journey of discovery and evolution—a journey that could transform not just relationships but entire communities and cultures.

The synthesis of her work in romantic revelation had revealed something fundamental: that true relationship wisdom came not from mastering relationship skills or achieving relationship goals but from developing the capacity to continuously reimagine and reconstruct romantic reality. In this understanding, Elena had not just achieved relationship innovation—she had opened new pathways for human romantic evolution and authentic connection.

Chapter 45: Economic Transformation

45.1 Radical Financial Reimagining

Elena Rodriguez's revolutionary insights into human potential had inevitably led her to confront one of society's most fundamental systems: the economic framework that shaped human possibility. Having transformed understanding of emotional and romantic consciousness, she now faced the challenge of reimagining economic structures to support genuine human flourishing.

The Economic Innovation Division at the Rodriguez Institute had evolved beyond traditional financial research—it had become a pioneering center for what Elena termed "economic consciousness transformation," exploring how financial systems could be fundamentally reimagined to support human potential. She recognized that true economic transformation required more than policy adjustments or market reforms. It demanded a complete reconceptualization of how economic systems could serve authentic human development and collective flourishing.

Dr. Michael Chang, leading the institute's economic research initiatives, recognized the revolutionary implications of Elena's approach. "What you're developing here," Michael observed during their strategy sessions, "isn't just another economic theory. It's a fundamental reimagining of how economic systems can support human potential."

The economic transformation frameworks Elena developed challenged conventional financial wisdom. Rather than focusing on traditional metrics of economic success, her methodologies centered on what she called "economic consciousness evolution"—the capacity for financial systems to support genuine human development and collective growth while maintaining stability and sustainability.

Her collaboration with international economic researchers had revealed surprising patterns in how financial structures both enabled and constrained human potential. These weren't just market patterns but deeply embedded frameworks that shaped how humans imagined and created their economic reality.

Dr. Sophia Rahman, heading the institute's financial innovation division, noted the unprecedented nature of Elena's work. "You're not just studying economic systems," she remarked. "You're creating entirely new possibilities for how financial structures can support human flourishing."

The methodologies Elena developed for economic transformation were extraordinary in their sophistication and scope. They combined cutting-edge financial theory with deep psychological insight, creating practical frameworks for reimagining economic structures while maintaining stability and promoting authentic human development.

45.2 Challenging Economic Limitations

Elena's approach to economic liberation transcended conventional notions of financial freedom or market reform. Her work revealed that true economic transformation required more than changing existing structures—it demanded the creation of entirely new frameworks for understanding and actualizing economic potential.

The International Center for Economic Innovation had become a hub for what Elena termed "constructive economic liberation"—approaches that didn't just challenge existing limitations but actively created new possibilities for human economic organization. These weren't just theoretical models but living experiments in how financial systems could support genuine human development.

Dr. James Wilson, overseeing global economic research initiatives, recognized the transformative potential of Elena's approach. "What we're witnessing," he noted, "is nothing less than a complete reimagining of how economic systems can serve human potential."

The liberation frameworks Elena developed were sophisticated systems that could adapt to different cultural and economic contexts while maintaining their core principles of human development. These weren't just financial reforms but comprehensive approaches to creating new possibilities for economic organization and human flourishing.

Her work with global economic researchers had expanded understanding of how financial transformation could occur across different cultural contexts. The patterns they discovered suggested universal principles underlying human potential for economic evolution while respecting cultural uniqueness and local needs.

Maria Gonzalez, collaborating on international economic initiatives, observed the unique nature of Elena's approach. "You've created something extraordinary," Maria remarked. "Not just methods for economic change, but entire ecosystems of financial possibility."

45.3 Wealth as a Catalyst for Change

The culmination of Elena's work in economic transformation revealed profound truths about human potential for financial evolution. This wasn't merely about changing economic systems; it was about fundamentally reimagining how wealth could serve as a catalyst for human development and collective flourishing.

Her research at the Rodriguez Institute had evolved into what she called "economic empowerment ecosystems"—comprehensive frameworks that supported continuous financial evolution while maintaining authentic human connection. These systems recognized that true economic empowerment came not from achieving fixed financial states but from developing the capacity for ongoing economic adaptation and growth.

Dr. Sarah Chen, leading international economic psychology initiatives, recognized the revolutionary nature of Elena's approach to financial transformation. "What Elena has developed," she noted, "is nothing less than a new paradigm for understanding how economic systems can support human potential."

The transformation methodologies she developed were sophisticated systems that could recognize and support unique cultural paths to economic evolution while maintaining connection to universal principles of human growth and authentic development. These weren't just financial tools but comprehensive frameworks for understanding human economic potential.

Her work with global research teams had revealed patterns in how communities achieved genuine economic transformation. These patterns suggested universal principles underlying human capacity for financial evolution while acknowledging the unique nature of different cultural and economic contexts.

David Kumar, observing the impact of Elena's work across various communities, noted its transformative potential. "You're not just helping economies change," he remarked. "You're showing them how to reimagine their entire relationship with economic possibility."

The frameworks Elena developed for economic transformation became living examples of what was possible in human financial development. Each application revealed new dimensions of potential, new ways of understanding how economic systems could support genuine human flourishing while maintaining authentic connection to cultural identity and collective growth.

Her approach to economic transformation had revealed something profound: that true financial evolution wasn't about achieving predetermined economic states but about developing the capacity for continuous adaptation and growth. The Rodriguez Economic Transformation Methodology, as it came to be known in financial circles, offered a new paradigm for understanding human potential for economic development.

As Elena reflected on the journey of economic transformation, she understood that this wasn't merely about changing financial systems or policies. It was about creating frameworks that could support continuous human economic evolution while maintaining authentic connection to psychological liberation and collective growth.

The catalyst for economic change, she had discovered, lay not in reaching fixed financial goals but in developing the capacity for ongoing economic evolution. Her work had shown that true financial transformation came from creating spaces where communities could continuously reimagine and reconstruct their relationship with economic possibility.

In the end, Elena Rodriguez had done more than develop new economic methodologies. She had created living frameworks for understanding and supporting human potential for continuous growth and transformation through financial systems. Her work suggested that economic transformation wasn't a destination but a continuous journey of discovery and evolution—a journey that could transform not just economies but entire societies and civilizations.

The synthesis of her work in economic transformation had revealed something fundamental: that true financial evolution came not from implementing new policies or reforms but from developing the capacity to continuously reimagine and reconstruct economic reality. In this understanding, Elena had not just achieved economic innovation—she had opened new pathways for human financial evolution and authentic development.

Chapter 46: Ethical Enlightenment

46.1 Developing Profound Moral Insight

Elena Rodriguez's revolutionary work in economic transformation had naturally led her to confront an even more fundamental domain: the ethical frameworks that underpinned all human systems and decisions. Having revolutionized understanding of economic potential, she now found herself drawn to explore the depths of human moral capacity and ethical consciousness.

The Ethics Research Division at the Rodriguez Institute had evolved beyond traditional moral philosophy—it had become a pioneering center for what Elena termed "ethical consciousness exploration," investigating the deepest layers of human moral potential. She recognized that true ethical sophistication required more than philosophical frameworks or moral guidelines. It demanded a complete reconceptualization of how humans could access and develop their innate capacity for moral wisdom.

Dr. Rachel Thompson, heading the institute's ethics research initiatives, recognized the groundbreaking nature of Elena's approach. "What you're uncovering here," Rachel observed during their analysis sessions, "isn't just another ethical theory. It's a fundamental reimagining of human moral potential."

The ethical insight frameworks Elena developed challenged conventional moral philosophy. Rather than focusing on traditional approaches to ethics, her methodologies centered on what she called "moral consciousness evolution"—the capacity for individuals and communities to access and integrate deeper levels of ethical understanding that transcended conventional moral reasoning.

Her collaboration with international ethics researchers had revealed surprising patterns in how moral insight both enabled and transformed human consciousness. These weren't just philosophical patterns but deeply embedded frameworks that shaped how humans accessed and integrated their capacity for ethical understanding.

Professor David Chen, leading the institute's moral development division, noted the unprecedented nature of Elena's discoveries. "You're not just studying ethical systems," he remarked. "You're uncovering entirely new dimensions of human capacity for moral wisdom."

The methodologies Elena developed for ethical exploration were extraordinary in their sophistication and depth. They combined cutting-edge moral psychology with profound philosophical insight, creating practical frameworks for accessing and integrating deeper levels of ethical understanding while maintaining psychological stability and promoting genuine human flourishing.

46.2 Navigating Complex Moral Landscapes

Elena's approach to moral complexity transcended conventional ethical frameworks and decision-making models. Her work revealed that true ethical navigation required more than applying moral principles—it demanded the ability to embrace and integrate increasingly complex ethical realities while maintaining authentic presence and moral integrity.

The International Center for Ethical Research had become a hub for what Elena termed "constructive moral complexity"—approaches that didn't just analyze ethical dilemmas but actively created new possibilities for moral understanding and integration. These weren't just theoretical models but living experiments in how humans could access and navigate deeper territories of ethical consciousness.

Dr. Maya Patel, overseeing global ethics research initiatives, recognized the transformative potential of Elena's approach. "What we're witnessing," she noted, "is nothing less than a complete reimagining of human capacity for moral wisdom."

The navigation frameworks Elena developed were sophisticated systems that could adapt to different cultural contexts while maintaining their core principles of ethical exploration. These weren't just decision-making tools but comprehensive approaches to creating new possibilities for moral understanding and integration.

Her work with global ethics researchers had expanded understanding of how moral complexity could be navigated across different cultural and philosophical contexts. The patterns they discovered suggested universal principles underlying human potential for ethical evolution while respecting individual and cultural uniqueness.

Dr. Sarah Williams, collaborating on international ethics initiatives, observed the unique nature of Elena's approach. "You've created something extraordinary," Sarah remarked. "Not just methods for moral reasoning, but entire ecosystems of ethical possibility."

46.3 The Refinement of Ethical Understanding

The culmination of Elena's work in ethical enlightenment revealed profound truths about human moral potential. This wasn't merely about developing better decision-making frameworks; it was about fundamentally reimagining what was possible in human ethical understanding and development.

Her research at the Rodriguez Institute had evolved into what she called "moral growth ecosystems"—comprehensive frameworks that supported continuous ethical evolution while maintaining authentic human connection. These systems recognized that true moral development came not from mastering fixed ethical principles but from developing the capacity for ongoing moral adaptation and integration.

Dr. Michael Wilson, leading international moral psychology initiatives, recognized the revolutionary nature of Elena's approach to ethical development. "What Elena has developed," he noted, "is nothing less than a new paradigm for understanding human moral potential."

The transformation methodologies she developed were sophisticated systems that could recognize and support unique individual paths to ethical evolution while maintaining connection to universal principles of human growth and authentic experience. These weren't just moral development tools but comprehensive frameworks for understanding human ethical potential.

Her work with global research teams had revealed patterns in how individuals and communities achieved genuine moral growth. These patterns suggested universal principles underlying human capacity for ethical evolution while acknowledging the unique nature of different cultural and philosophical contexts.

Isabella Martinez, observing the impact of Elena's work across various communities, noted its transformative potential. "You're not just helping people make better decisions," she remarked. "You're showing them how to reimagine their entire relationship with moral possibility."

The frameworks Elena developed for ethical understanding became living examples of what was possible in human moral development. Each application revealed new dimensions of potential, new ways of understanding how humans could achieve genuine ethical sophistication while maintaining authentic connection to individual growth and cultural identity.

Her approach to ethical enlightenment had revealed something profound: that true moral development wasn't about mastering predetermined ethical principles but about developing the capacity for continuous moral evolution. The Rodriguez Ethical Development Methodology, as it came to be known in philosophical circles, offered a new paradigm for understanding human potential for moral transformation.

As Elena reflected on the journey of ethical enlightenment, she understood that this wasn't merely about improving decision-making or developing moral guidelines. It was about creating frameworks that could support continuous human moral evolution while maintaining authentic connection to psychological liberation and individual growth.

The refinement of ethical understanding, she had discovered, lay not in reaching fixed moral conclusions but in developing the capacity for ongoing ethical evolution. Her work had shown that true moral growth came from creating spaces where individuals could continuously reimagine and reconstruct their relationship with ethical possibility.

In the end, Elena Rodriguez had done more than develop new ethical methodologies. She had created living frameworks for understanding and supporting human potential for continuous growth and transformation through moral development. Her work suggested that ethical enlightenment wasn't a destination but a continuous journey of discovery and evolution—a journey that could transform not just individuals but entire communities and cultures.

The synthesis of her work in ethical enlightenment had revealed something fundamental: that true moral development came not from mastering ethical principles or achieving moral certainty but from developing the capacity to continuously reimagine and reconstruct ethical reality. In this understanding, Elena had not just achieved philosophical innovation—she had opened new pathways for human moral evolution and authentic connection.

Chapter 47: Intellectual Transcendence

47.1 Expanding Intellectual Horizons

Elena Rodriguez's groundbreaking work in ethical enlightenment had naturally led her to explore its cognitive foundation: the vast territory of human intellectual potential. Having revolutionized understanding of moral consciousness, she now found herself drawn to investigate the furthest reaches of human intellectual capacity and understanding.

The Cognitive Research Division at the Rodriguez Institute had evolved beyond traditional intellectual studies—it had become a pioneering center for what Elena termed "intellectual consciousness exploration," investigating the outermost boundaries of human cognitive potential. She recognized that true intellectual breakthrough required more than academic knowledge or analytical skill. It demanded a complete reconceptualization of how humans could access and develop their innate capacity for profound understanding.

Dr. Alexander Chen, heading the institute's cognitive research initiatives, recognized the revolutionary implications of Elena's approach. "What you're discovering here," Alexander observed during their research sessions, "isn't just another theory of intelligence. It's a fundamental reimagining of human intellectual potential."

The intellectual breakthrough frameworks Elena developed challenged conventional cognitive science. Rather than focusing on traditional metrics of intelligence, her methodologies centered on what she called "cognitive consciousness evolution"—the capacity for individuals to access and integrate deeper levels of understanding that transcended conventional intellectual boundaries.

Her collaboration with international cognitive researchers had revealed surprising patterns in how intellectual breakthrough both enabled and transformed human consciousness. These weren't just cognitive patterns but deeply embedded frameworks that shaped how humans accessed and integrated their capacity for profound understanding.

Professor Maria Santos, leading the institute's intellectual development division, noted the unprecedented nature of Elena's discoveries. "You're not just studying cognitive processes," she remarked. "You're uncovering entirely new dimensions of human capacity for intellectual achievement."

The methodologies Elena developed for intellectual exploration were extraordinary in their sophistication and depth. They combined cutting-edge neuroscience with profound psychological insight, creating practical frameworks for accessing and integrating deeper levels of understanding while maintaining psychological balance and promoting genuine human flourishing.

47.2 Challenging Fundamental Intellectual Boundaries

Elena's approach to intellectual boundaries transcended conventional notions of academic achievement or cognitive development. Her work revealed that true intellectual revolution required more than expanding knowledge—it demanded the ability to transcend established cognitive frameworks while maintaining authentic connection to practical wisdom.

The International Center for Cognitive Research had become a hub for what Elena termed "constructive intellectual revolution"—approaches that didn't just challenge existing cognitive limitations but actively created new possibilities for human understanding. These weren't just theoretical models but living experiments in how humans could access and navigate deeper territories of intellectual experience.

Dr. James Wilson, overseeing global cognitive research initiatives, recognized the transformative potential of Elena's approach. "What we're witnessing," he noted, "is nothing less than a complete reimagining of human capacity for intellectual advancement."

The revolutionary frameworks Elena developed were sophisticated systems that could adapt to different cultural and educational contexts while maintaining their core principles of intellectual exploration. These weren't just learning tools but comprehensive approaches to creating new possibilities for cognitive development and integration.

Her work with global cognitive researchers had expanded understanding of how intellectual boundaries could be transcended across different cultural and psychological contexts. The patterns they discovered suggested universal principles underlying human potential for intellectual evolution while respecting individual and cultural uniqueness.

Dr. Sarah Thompson, collaborating on international cognitive initiatives, observed the unique nature of Elena's approach. "You've created something extraordinary," Sarah remarked. "Not just methods for intellectual development, but entire ecosystems of cognitive possibility."

47.3 The Pursuit of Intellectual Enlightenment

The culmination of Elena's work in intellectual transcendence revealed profound truths about human cognitive potential. This wasn't merely about acquiring knowledge or developing skills; it was about fundamentally reimagining what was possible in human intellectual development and understanding.

Her research at the Rodriguez Institute had evolved into what she called "cognitive enlightenment ecosystems"—comprehensive frameworks that supported continuous intellectual evolution while maintaining authentic human connection. These systems recognized that true intellectual enlightenment came not from mastering fixed bodies of knowledge but from developing the capacity for ongoing cognitive adaptation and integration.

Dr. Michael Patel, leading international cognitive psychology initiatives, recognized the revolutionary nature of Elena's approach to intellectual development. "What Elena has developed," he noted, "is nothing less than a new paradigm for understanding human intellectual potential."

The transformation methodologies she developed were sophisticated systems that could recognize and support unique individual paths to intellectual enlightenment while maintaining connection to universal principles of human growth and authentic experience. These weren't just learning tools but comprehensive frameworks for understanding human cognitive potential.

Her work with global research teams had revealed patterns in how individuals achieved genuine intellectual breakthroughs. These patterns suggested universal principles underlying human capacity for cognitive evolution while acknowledging the unique nature of individual learning contexts.

Isabella Chen, observing the impact of Elena's work across various communities, noted its transformative potential. "You're not just helping people learn," she remarked. "You're showing them how to reimagine their entire relationship with intellectual possibility."

The frameworks Elena developed for intellectual enlightenment became living examples of what was possible in human cognitive development. Each application revealed new dimensions of potential, new ways of understanding how humans could achieve genuine intellectual transcendence while maintaining authentic connection to individual growth and cultural identity.

Her approach to intellectual transcendence had revealed something profound: that true cognitive development wasn't about mastering predetermined bodies of knowledge but about developing the capacity for continuous intellectual evolution. The Rodriguez Cognitive Development Methodology, as it came to be known in academic circles, offered a new paradigm for understanding human potential for intellectual transformation.

As Elena reflected on the journey of intellectual transcendence, she understood that this wasn't merely about improving cognitive abilities or expanding knowledge. It was about creating frameworks that could support continuous human intellectual evolution while maintaining authentic connection to psychological liberation and individual growth.

The pursuit of intellectual enlightenment, she had discovered, lay not in reaching fixed cognitive goals but in developing the capacity for ongoing intellectual evolution. Her work had shown that true cognitive growth came from creating spaces where individuals could continuously reimagine and reconstruct their relationship with intellectual possibility.

In the end, Elena Rodriguez had done more than develop new learning methodologies. She had created living frameworks for understanding and supporting human potential for continuous growth and transformation through intellectual development. Her work suggested that intellectual transcendence wasn't a destination but a continuous journey of discovery and evolution—a journey that could transform not just individuals but entire communities and cultures.

The synthesis of her work in intellectual transcendence had revealed something fundamental: that true cognitive development came not from mastering knowledge or achieving intellectual certainty but from developing the capacity to continuously reimagine and reconstruct cognitive reality. In this understanding, Elena had not just achieved educational innovation—she had opened new pathways for human intellectual evolution and authentic understanding.

Chapter 48: Personal Synthesis

48.1 Integrating Personal Transformations

Elena Rodriguez's revolutionary work in intellectual transcendence had naturally evolved toward its ultimate expression: the complete integration of all dimensions of human potential. Having transformed understanding of cognitive development, she now faced the challenge of synthesizing the full spectrum of human experience into a coherent whole.

The Personal Integration Division at the Rodriguez Institute had evolved beyond traditional psychological research—it had become a pioneering center for what Elena termed "holistic consciousness synthesis," exploring how individuals could fully integrate their various dimensions of growth and transformation. She recognized that true self-realization required more than individual developments in separate domains. It demanded a complete reconceptualization of how humans could achieve genuine wholeness and authentic integration.

Dr. Sarah Chen, leading the institute's integration research initiatives, recognized the profound implications of Elena's approach. "What you're developing here," Sarah observed during their synthesis sessions, "isn't just another theory of personal development. It's a fundamental reimagining of human potential for complete integration."

The personal synthesis frameworks Elena developed challenged conventional psychology. Rather than focusing on separate aspects of human development, her methodologies centered on what she called "consciousness integration evolution"—the capacity for individuals to achieve genuine wholeness by harmoniously integrating all dimensions of their being and experience.

Her collaboration with international integration researchers had revealed surprising patterns in how personal synthesis both enabled and transformed human consciousness. These weren't just psychological patterns but deeply embedded frameworks that shaped how humans achieved authentic wholeness and integration.

Professor David Kumar, heading the institute's personal development division, noted the unprecedented nature of Elena's discoveries. "You're not just studying personal growth," he remarked. "You're uncovering entirely new possibilities for human integration and wholeness."

The methodologies Elena developed for personal synthesis were extraordinary in their sophistication and scope. They combined insights from all domains of human development—emotional, intellectual, spiritual, and social—creating practical frameworks for achieving genuine integration while maintaining authentic individual expression.

48.2 Harmonizing Internal Complexities

Elena's approach to personal balance transcended conventional notions of psychological harmony or life balance. Her work revealed that true internal harmony required more than managing different aspects of life—it demanded the ability to achieve genuine integration while maintaining the unique character of each dimension of human experience.

The International Center for Personal Integration had become a hub for what Elena termed "constructive complexity harmony"—approaches that didn't just balance different aspects of life but actively created new possibilities for genuine personal integration. These weren't just theoretical models but living experiments in how humans could achieve authentic wholeness.

Dr. Maya Patel, overseeing global integration research initiatives, recognized the transformative potential of Elena's approach. "What we're witnessing," she noted, "is nothing less than a complete reimagining of how humans can achieve genuine personal harmony."

The harmonization frameworks Elena developed were sophisticated systems that could adapt to different individual contexts while maintaining their core principles of integration. These weren't just balance techniques but comprehensive approaches to creating new possibilities for personal wholeness and authentic expression.

Her work with global researchers had expanded understanding of how personal harmony could be achieved across different cultural and psychological contexts. The patterns they discovered suggested universal principles underlying human potential for integration while respecting individual uniqueness and cultural diversity.

Dr. Isabella Martinez, collaborating on international integration initiatives, observed the unique nature of Elena's approach. "You've created something extraordinary," Isabella remarked. "Not just methods for achieving balance, but entire ecosystems of personal harmony."

48.3 The Journey of Holistic Self-Understanding

The culmination of Elena's work in personal synthesis revealed profound truths about human potential for complete integration. This wasn't merely about balancing different aspects of life; it was about fundamentally reimagining what was possible in human wholeness and authentic self-realization.

Her research at the Rodriguez Institute had evolved into what she called "wisdom integration ecosystems"—comprehensive frameworks that supported continuous personal evolution while maintaining authentic wholeness. These systems recognized that true personal wisdom came not from achieving fixed states of balance but from developing the capacity for ongoing integration and authentic expression.

Dr. Michael Wilson, leading international psychology initiatives, recognized the revolutionary nature of Elena's approach to personal wisdom. "What Elena has developed," he noted, "is nothing less than a new paradigm for understanding human potential for complete integration."

The synthesis methodologies she developed were sophisticated systems that could recognize and support unique individual paths to wisdom while maintaining connection to universal principles of human integration. These weren't just personal development tools but comprehensive frameworks for understanding human potential for authentic wholeness.

Her work with global research teams had revealed patterns in how individuals achieved genuine personal wisdom. These patterns suggested universal principles underlying human capacity for integration while acknowledging the unique nature of individual life contexts.

Rachel Thompson, observing the impact of Elena's work across various communities, noted its transformative potential. "You're not just helping people achieve balance," she remarked. "You're showing them how to reimagine their entire relationship with personal wholeness."

The frameworks Elena developed for personal wisdom became living examples of what was possible in human integration. Each application revealed new dimensions of potential, new ways of understanding how humans could achieve genuine wholeness while maintaining authentic expression of their unique nature.

Her approach to personal synthesis had revealed something profound: that true integration wasn't about achieving predetermined states of balance but about developing the capacity for continuous personal evolution. The Rodriguez Integration Methodology, as it came to be known in psychological circles, offered a new paradigm for understanding human potential for complete transformation.

As Elena reflected on the journey of personal synthesis, she understood that this wasn't merely about harmonizing different aspects of life. It was about creating frameworks that could support continuous human evolution while maintaining authentic connection to all dimensions of experience.

The journey of holistic self-understanding, she had discovered, lay not in reaching fixed states of integration but in developing the capacity for ongoing personal evolution. Her work had shown that true wisdom came from creating spaces where individuals could continuously reimagine and reconstruct their relationship with personal wholeness.

In the end, Elena Rodriguez had done more than develop new integration methodologies. She had created living frameworks for understanding and supporting human potential for continuous growth and transformation through complete personal synthesis. Her work suggested that personal wisdom wasn't a destination but a continuous journey of discovery and evolution—a journey that could transform not just individuals but entire communities and cultures.

The synthesis of her work in personal integration had revealed something fundamental: that true wholeness came not from achieving balance or harmony but from developing the capacity to continuously reimagine and reconstruct personal reality. In this understanding, Elena had not just achieved psychological innovation—she had opened new pathways for human integration and authentic expression.

Chapter 49: Romantic Synthesis

49.1 Harmonizing Romantic Perspectives

Elena Rodriguez's groundbreaking work in personal synthesis had naturally led her to explore its most profound interpersonal expression: the complete integration of romantic connection. Having transformed understanding of individual wholeness, she now found herself drawn to investigate how this integration manifested in intimate relationships.

The Relationship Synthesis Division at the Rodriguez Institute had evolved beyond traditional couple's research—it had become a pioneering center for what Elena termed "romantic consciousness integration," exploring how intimate relationships could achieve genuine wholeness and authentic harmony. She recognized that true relationship integration required more than communication skills or compatibility. It demanded a complete reconceptualization of how two individuals could achieve genuine unity while maintaining authentic individuality.

Dr. Maya Williams, heading the institute's relationship integration initiatives, recognized the revolutionary implications of Elena's approach. "What you're uncovering here," Maya observed during their analysis sessions, "isn't just another theory of relationship dynamics. It's a fundamental reimagining of human potential for complete romantic integration."

The relationship synthesis frameworks Elena developed challenged conventional couples psychology. Rather than focusing on problem-solving or communication techniques, her methodologies centered on what she called "romantic consciousness evolution"—the capacity for relationships to achieve genuine wholeness through the harmonious integration of both partners' complete being.

Her collaboration with international relationship researchers had revealed surprising patterns in how romantic integration both enabled and transformed human consciousness. These weren't just psychological patterns but deeply embedded frameworks that shaped how couples achieved authentic wholeness and mutual growth.

Professor James Chen, leading the institute's relationship development division, noted the unprecedented nature of Elena's discoveries. "You're not just studying relationships," he remarked. "You're uncovering entirely new possibilities for human connection and romantic wholeness."

The methodologies Elena developed for romantic integration were extraordinary in their sophistication and depth. They combined insights from all domains of human connection—emotional, intellectual, spiritual, and physical—creating practical frameworks for achieving genuine relationship synthesis while maintaining authentic individual expression.

49.2 Navigating Profound Emotional Connections

Elena's approach to romantic depth transcended conventional notions of emotional intimacy or relationship development. Her work revealed that true romantic synthesis required more than deep connection—it demanded the ability to achieve genuine integration of all aspects of both partners' beings while maintaining their unique essences.

The International Center for Relationship Research had become a hub for what Elena termed "constructive romantic synthesis"—approaches that didn't just deepen connections but actively created new possibilities for complete relationship integration. These weren't just theoretical models but living experiments in how couples could achieve authentic wholeness.

Dr. Sarah Patel, overseeing global relationship research initiatives, recognized the transformative potential of Elena's approach. "What we're witnessing," she noted, "is nothing less than a complete reimagining of how romantic relationships can achieve genuine synthesis."

The integration frameworks Elena developed were sophisticated systems that could adapt to different relationship contexts while maintaining their core principles of romantic wholeness. These weren't just relationship tools but comprehensive approaches to creating new possibilities for intimate connection and mutual growth.

Her work with global researchers had expanded understanding of how romantic depth could be achieved across different cultural and psychological contexts. The patterns they discovered suggested universal principles underlying human potential for relationship integration while respecting individual and cultural uniqueness.

Dr. Isabella Thompson, collaborating on international relationship initiatives, observed the unique nature of Elena's approach. "You've created something extraordinary," Isabella remarked. "Not just methods for deepening connection, but entire ecosystems of romantic possibility."

49.3 Love as a Unifying Force

The culmination of Elena's work in romantic synthesis revealed profound truths about human potential for complete relationship integration. This wasn't merely about achieving deeper connection; it was about fundamentally reimagining what was possible in human romantic wholeness and mutual transformation.

Her research at the Rodriguez Institute had evolved into what she called "love integration ecosystems"—comprehensive frameworks that supported continuous relationship evolution while maintaining authentic individual expression. These systems recognized that true romantic synthesis came not from achieving fixed states of connection but from developing the capacity for ongoing mutual growth and integration.

Dr. Michael Kumar, leading international relationship psychology initiatives, recognized the revolutionary nature of Elena's approach to romantic synthesis. "What Elena has developed," he noted, "is nothing less than a new paradigm for understanding human potential for complete relationship integration."

The synthesis methodologies she developed were sophisticated systems that could recognize and support unique relationship paths to wholeness while maintaining connection to universal principles of human growth. These weren't just relationship development tools but comprehensive frameworks for understanding human potential for romantic integration.

Her work with global research teams had revealed patterns in how couples achieved genuine relationship synthesis. These patterns suggested universal principles underlying human capacity for romantic integration while acknowledging the unique nature of each relationship context.

Rachel Martinez, observing the impact of Elena's work across various communities, noted its transformative potential. "You're not just helping couples connect," she remarked. "You're showing them how to reimagine their entire relationship with romantic possibility."

The frameworks Elena developed for romantic synthesis became living examples of what was possible in relationship integration. Each application revealed new dimensions of potential, new ways of understanding how couples could achieve genuine wholeness while maintaining authentic expression of their individual natures.

Her approach to romantic synthesis had revealed something profound: that true relationship integration wasn't about achieving predetermined states of connection but about developing the capacity for continuous mutual evolution. The Rodriguez Relationship Synthesis Methodology, as it came to be known in psychological circles, offered a new paradigm for understanding human potential for complete romantic transformation.

As Elena reflected on the journey of romantic synthesis, she understood that this wasn't merely about deepening connection or improving communication. It was about creating frameworks that could support continuous relationship evolution while maintaining authentic expression of both partners' complete being.

The power of love as a unifying force, she had discovered, lay not in reaching fixed states of connection but in developing the capacity for ongoing mutual evolution. Her work had shown that true romantic synthesis came from creating spaces where couples could continuously reimagine and reconstruct their relationship with intimate possibility.

In the end, Elena Rodriguez had done more than develop new relationship methodologies. She had created living frameworks for understanding and supporting human potential for continuous growth and transformation through complete romantic integration. Her work suggested that relationship synthesis wasn't a destination but a continuous journey of discovery and evolution—a journey that could transform not just couples but entire communities and cultures.

The synthesis of her work in romantic integration had revealed something fundamental: that true relationship wholeness came not from achieving connection or harmony but from developing the capacity to continuously reimagine and reconstruct romantic reality. In this understanding, Elena had not just achieved relationship innovation—she had opened new pathways for human romantic evolution and authentic mutual transformation.

Chapter 50: Ultimate Transformation

50.1 The Culmination of Personal Journey

The Rodriguez Institute's final breakthrough in human potential came not as a singular discovery but as a profound synthesis of all that had come before. Dr. Elena Rodriguez, standing at the threshold of what she termed "complete human integration," found herself contemplating the extraordinary journey that had led to this moment of ultimate transformation.

The Total Transformation Division, operating at the cutting edge of human potential research, had evolved beyond traditional paradigms of personal development. Under Elena's guidance, it had become a pioneering center for what she called "complete consciousness integration"—a state where all aspects of human potential could achieve perfect harmony and expression.

Dr. Marcus Chen, leading the institute's culmination studies, recognized the revolutionary nature of their findings. "What we're witnessing," he observed during their final analysis sessions, "isn't just another step in human evolution. It's a fundamental reimagining of human potential itself."

The transformation frameworks Elena had developed challenged every conventional understanding of human capability. Rather than focusing on incremental improvements or specific skills, her methodologies centered on what she termed "consciousness evolution"—the capacity for humans to achieve complete integration of all aspects of their being.

Her collaboration with international researchers had revealed unprecedented patterns in how human consciousness could evolve beyond previously imagined limitations. These weren't just psychological or spiritual patterns but fundamental frameworks that shaped the very nature of human potential and growth.

Professor Sarah Williams, overseeing the institute's integration initiatives, noted the extraordinary implications of Elena's discoveries. "You've uncovered something beyond transformation," she remarked. "You've revealed pathways to complete human actualization that we never knew existed."

The methodologies Elena developed for total transformation were revolutionary in their comprehensiveness and depth. They combined insights from all domains of human experience—physical, emotional, intellectual, and spiritual—creating practical frameworks for achieving genuine wholeness while maintaining authentic individual expression.

50.2 Transcending All Previous Limitations

Elena's approach to ultimate liberation transcended conventional notions of human potential and personal growth. Her work revealed that true transformation required more than overcoming limitations—it demanded a complete reconceptualization of what was possible in human experience and development.

The International Center for Human Potential had become a hub for what Elena termed "constructive consciousness evolution"—approaches that didn't just break through limitations but actively created new possibilities for human expression and growth. These weren't just theoretical models but living experiments in human potential.

Dr. James Thompson, directing global transformation research, recognized the unprecedented nature of Elena's approach. "What we're discovering," he noted, "is nothing less than a complete reimagining of human capability and potential."

The liberation frameworks Elena developed were sophisticated systems that could adapt to different individual contexts while maintaining their core principles of complete transformation. These weren't just personal development tools but comprehensive approaches to creating new possibilities for human evolution and growth.

Her work with global researchers had expanded understanding of how ultimate liberation could be achieved across different cultural and psychological contexts. The patterns they discovered suggested universal principles underlying human potential for complete transformation while respecting individual and cultural uniqueness.

Dr. Maya Patel, collaborating on international transformation initiatives, observed the revolutionary nature of Elena's approach. "You've created something extraordinary," Maya remarked. "Not just methods for overcoming limitations, but entire ecosystems of human possibility."

50.3 The Realization of Complete Potential

The culmination of Elena's work in human transformation revealed profound truths about human potential for complete integration and actualization. This wasn't merely about achieving personal growth; it was about fundamentally reimagining what was possible in human consciousness and development.

Her research at the Rodriguez Institute had evolved into what she called "consciousness integration ecosystems"—comprehensive frameworks that supported continuous evolution while maintaining authentic individual expression. These systems recognized that true transformation came not from achieving fixed states but from developing the capacity for ongoing growth and integration.

Dr. David Kumar, leading international consciousness research initiatives, recognized the revolutionary nature of Elena's approach to human potential. "What Elena has developed," he noted, "is nothing less than a new paradigm for understanding human capacity for complete transformation."

The transformation methodologies she developed were sophisticated systems that could recognize and support unique individual paths to wholeness while maintaining connection to universal principles of human growth. These weren't just personal development tools but comprehensive frameworks for understanding human potential for complete integration.

Her work with global research teams had revealed patterns in how individuals achieved genuine transformation. These patterns suggested universal principles underlying human capacity for complete integration while acknowledging the unique nature of each individual's journey.

Rachel Martinez, observing the impact of Elena's work across various communities, noted its transformative potential. "You're not just helping people grow," she remarked. "You're showing them how to reimagine their entire relationship with human possibility."

The frameworks Elena developed for ultimate transformation became living examples of what was possible in human development. Each application revealed new dimensions of potential, new ways of understanding how individuals could achieve genuine wholeness while maintaining authentic expression of their unique nature.

Her approach to complete transformation had revealed something profound: that true human potential wasn't about achieving predetermined states but about developing the capacity for continuous evolution. The Rodriguez Transformation Methodology, as it came to be known in scientific circles, offered a new paradigm for understanding human capacity for complete actualization.

As Elena reflected on the journey of human transformation, she understood that this wasn't merely about personal growth or development. It was about creating frameworks that could support continuous human evolution while maintaining authentic expression of each individual's complete being.

The power of transformation, she had discovered, lay not in reaching fixed states of development but in developing the capacity for ongoing evolution. Her work had shown that true human potential came from creating spaces where individuals could continuously reimagine and reconstruct their relationship with possibility.

In the end, Elena Rodriguez had done more than develop new transformation methodologies. She had created living frameworks for understanding and supporting human potential for continuous growth and evolution. Her work suggested that transformation wasn't a destination but a continuous journey of discovery and evolution—a journey that could transform not just individuals but entire communities and cultures.

The synthesis of her work in human transformation had revealed something fundamental: that true human potential came not from achieving growth or development but from developing the capacity to continuously reimagine and reconstruct human reality. In this understanding, Elena had not just achieved scientific innovation—she had opened new pathways for human evolution and authentic transformation.

As the Rodriguez Institute prepared to share these final discoveries with the world, Elena understood that this wasn't an ending but a beginning. The frameworks she had developed weren't just tools for personal transformation—they were keys to unlocking entirely new dimensions of human potential and possibility.

The journey of complete transformation, she realized, would continue long after her own work was done. What she had created were not just methodologies but living systems that could evolve and adapt, supporting endless generations in their journey toward complete actualization and authentic expression of human potential.

In this final chapter of her research, Elena Rodriguez had not just documented transformation—she had created pathways for ongoing human evolution that would continue to reveal new possibilities for generations to come. The ultimate transformation, she understood, was not a final state but an eternal process of becoming, an endless journey into the expanding horizon of human potential.

www.ingramcontent.com/pod-product-compliance
Lightning Source LLC
LaVergne TN
LVHW010052170826
845678LV00012B/2119

* 9 7 9 8 2 3 0 8 0 2 8 9 1 *